Alcibiades

Part I & II

Plato

1st WORLD
LIBRARY
Literary Society

Alcibiades I and II
Plato
Translated by Benjamin Jowett

© 1st World Library – Literary Society, 2004
PO Box 2211
Fairfield, IA 52556
www.1stworldlibrary.org
First Edition

LCCN: 2003195119

ISBN : 1-59540-444-9

Purchase *"Alcibiades I & II"*
as a traditional bound book at:
www.1stWorldLibrary.org/purchase.asp?ISBN=1-59540-444-9

1st World Library Literary Society is a nonprofit
organization dedicated to promoting literacy by:

- Creating a free internet library accessible from
  any computer worldwide.
- Hosting writing competitions and offering book
  publishing scholarships.

Readers interested in supporting literacy
through sponsorship, donations or
membership please contact:
literacy@1stworldlibrary.org
Check us out at: www.1stworldlibrary.org

Contents

INTRODUCTION.

The First Alcibiades is a conversation between Socrates and Alcibiades. Socrates is represented in the character which he attributes to himself in the Apology of a know-nothing who detects the conceit of knowledge in others. The two have met already in the Protagoras and in the Symposium; in the latter dialogue, as in this, the relation between them is that of a lover and his beloved. But the narrative of their loves is told differently in different places; for in the Symposium Alcibiades is depicted as the impassioned but rejected lover; here, as coldly receiving the advances of Socrates, who, for the best of purposes, lies in wait for the aspiring and ambitious youth.

Alcibiades, who is described as a very young man, is about to enter on public life, having an inordinate opinion of himself, and an extravagant ambition. Socrates, 'who knows what is in man,' astonishes him by a revelation of his designs. But has he the knowledge which is necessary for carrying them out? He is going to persuade the Athenians - about what?

Not about any particular art, but about politics - when to fight and when to make peace. Now, men should fight and make peace on just grounds, and therefore the question of justice and injustice must enter into peace and war; and he who advises the Athenians must know the difference between them. Does Alcibiades know? If he does, he must either have been taught by some master, or he must have discovered the nature of them himself. If he has had a master, Socrates would like to be informed who he is, that he may go and learn of him also. Alcibiades admits that he has never learned. Then has he enquired for himself? He may have, if he was ever aware of a time when he was ignorant. But he never was ignorant; for when he played with other boys at dice, he charged them with cheating, and this implied a knowledge of just and unjust. According to his own explanation, he had learned of the multitude. Why, he asks, should he not learn of them the nature of justice, as he has learned the Greek language of them? To this Socrates answers, that they can teach Greek, but they cannot teach justice; for they are agreed about the one, but they are not agreed about the other: and therefore Alcibiades, who has admitted that if he knows he must either have learned from a master or have discovered for himself the nature of justice, is convicted out of his own mouth.

Alcibiades rejoins, that the Athenians debate not about what is just, but about what is expedient; and he asserts that the two principles of justice and expediency are opposed. Socrates, by a series of questions, compels him to admit that the just and the expedient coincide. Alcibiades is thus reduced to the humiliating conclusion that he knows nothing of politics, even if, as he says, they are concerned with the expedient.

However, he is no worse than other Athenian statesmen; and he will not need training, for others are as ignorant as he is. He is reminded that he has to contend, not only with his own countrymen, but with their enemies—with the Spartan kings and with the great king of Persia; and he can only attain this higher aim of ambition by the assistance of Socrates. Not that Socrates himself professes to have attained the truth, but the questions which he asks bring others to a knowledge of themselves, and this is the first step in the practice of virtue.

The dialogue continues: - We wish to become as good as possible. But to be good in what? Alcibiades replies - 'Good in transacting business.' But what business? 'The business of the most intelligent men at Athens.' The cobbler is intelligent in shoemaking, and is therefore good in that; he is not intelligent, and therefore not good, in weaving. Is he good in the sense which Alcibiades means, who is also bad? 'I mean,' replies Alcibiades, 'the man who is able to command in the city.' But to command what - horses or men? and if men, under what circumstances? 'I mean to say, that he is able to command men living in social and political relations.' And what is their aim? 'The better preservation of the city.' But when is a city better? 'When there is unanimity, such as exists between husband and wife.' Then, when husbands and wives perform their own special duties, there can be no unanimity between them; nor can a city be well ordered when each citizen does his own work only. Alcibiades, having stated first that goodness consists in the unanimity of the citizens, and then in each of them doing his own separate work, is brought to the required point of self-contradiction, leading him to confess his own ignorance.

But he is not too old to learn, and may still arrive at the truth, if he is willing to be cross-examined by Socrates. He must know himself; that is to say, not his body, or the things of the body, but his mind, or truer self. The physician knows the body, and the tradesman knows his own business, but they do not necessarily know themselves. Self-knowledge can be obtained only by looking into the mind and virtue of the soul, which is the diviner part of a man, as we see our own image in another's eye. And if we do not know ourselves, we cannot know what belongs to ourselves or belongs to others, and are unfit to take a part in political affairs. Both for the sake of the individual and of the state, we ought to aim at justice and temperance, not at wealth or power. The evil and unjust should have no power, - they should be the slaves of better men than themselves. None but the virtuous are deserving of freedom.

And are you, Alcibiades, a freeman? 'I feel that I am not; but I hope, Socrates, that by your aid I may become free, and from this day forward I will never leave you.'

The Alcibiades has several points of resemblance to the undoubted dialogues of Plato. The process of interrogation is of the same kind with that which Socrates practises upon the youthful Cleinias in the Euthydemus; and he characteristically attributes to Alcibiades the answers which he has elicited from him. The definition of good is narrowed by successive questions, and virtue is shown to be identical with knowledge. Here, as elsewhere, Socrates awakens the conscious-ness not of sin but of ignorance. Self-humiliation is the first step to knowledge, even of the commonest things. No man knows how ignorant he is, and no man can arrive at virtue and wisdom who has not once in his life, at least, been convicted of error. The process by which the soul is elevated is not unlike that which religious writers describe under the name of 'conversion,' if we substitute the sense of ignorance for the consciousness of sin.

In some respects the dialogue differs from any other Platonic composition. The aim is more directly ethical and hortatory; the process by which the antagonist is undermined is simpler than in other Platonic writings, and the concl-usion more decided. There is a good deal of humour in the manner in which the pride of Alcibiades, and of the Greeks generally, is supposed to be taken down by the Spartan and Persian queens; and the dialogue has considerable dialectical merit. But we have a difficulty in supposing that the same writer, who has given so profound and complex a notion of the characters both of Alcibiades and Socrates in the Symposium, should have treated them in so thin and superficial a manner in the Alcibiades, or that he would have ascribed to the ironical Socrates the rather unmeaning boast that Alcibiades could not attain the objects of his ambition without his help; or that he should have imagined that a mighty nature like his could have been reformed by a few not very conclusive words of Socrates. For the arguments by which Alcibiades is reformed are not convincing; the writer of the dialogue, whoever he was, arrives at his idealism by crooked and tortuous paths, in which many pitfalls are concealed. The anachronism of making Alcibiades about twenty years old during the life of his uncle, Pericles, may be noted; and the repetition of the favourite observation, which occurs also in the Laches and Protagoras, that great Athenian statesmen, like Pericles, failed in the education of their sons. There is none of the undoubted dialogues of Plato in which there is so little dramatic verisimilitude.

ALCIBIADES I

(see Appendix I)

PERSONS OF THE DIALOGUE: Alcibiades, Socrates

SOCRATES: I dare say that you may be surprised to find, O son of Cleinias, that I, who am your first lover, not having spoken to you for many years, when the rest of the world were wearying you with their attentions, am the last of your lovers who still speaks to you. The cause of my silence has been that I was hindered by a power more than human, of which I will some day explain to you the nature; this impediment has now been removed; I therefore here present myself before you, and I greatly hope that no similar hindrance will again occur. Meanwhile, I have observed that your pride has been too much for the pride of your admirers; they were numerous and high-spirited, but they have all run away, overpowered by your superior force of character; not one of them remains. And I want you to understand the reason why you have been too much for them.

You think that you have no need of them or of any other man, for you have great possessions and lack nothing, beginning with the body, and ending with the soul. In the first place, you say to yourself that you are the fairest and tallest of the citizens, and this every one who has eyes may see to be true; in the second place, that you are among the noblest of them, highly connected both on the father's and the mother's side, and sprung from one of the most distinguished families in your own state, which is the greatest in Hellas, and having many friends and kinsmen of the best sort, who can assist you when in need; and there is one potent relative, who is more to you than all the rest, Pericles the son of Xanthippus, whom your father left guardian of you, and of your brother, and who can do as he pleases not only in this city, but in all Hellas, and among many and mighty barbarous nations. Moreover, you are rich; but I must say that you value yourself least of all upon your possessions. And all these things have lifted you up; you have overcome your lovers, and they have acknowledged that you were too much for them. Have you not remarked their absence? And now I know that you wonder why I, unlike the rest of them, have not gone away, and what can be my motive in remaining.

ALCIBIADES: Perhaps, Socrates, you are not aware that I was just going to ask you the very same question - What do you want? And what is your motive in annoying me, and always, wherever I am, making a point of coming? (Compare Symp.) I do really wonder what you mean, and should greatly like to know.

SOCRATES: Then if, as you say, you desire to know, I suppose that you will be willing to hear, and I may consider myself to be speaking to an auditor who will remain, and will not run away?

ALCIBIADES: Certainly, let me hear.

SOCRATES: You had better be careful, for I may very likely be as unwilling to end as I have hitherto been to begin.

ALCIBIADES: Proceed, my good man, and I will listen.

SOCRATES: I will proceed; and, although no lover likes to speak with one who has no feeling of love in him (compare Symp.), I will make an effort, and tell you what I meant: My love, Alcibiades, which I hardly like to confess, would long ago have passed away, as I flatter myself, if I saw you loving your good things, or thinking that you ought to pass life in the enjoyment of them. But I shall reveal other thoughts of yours, which you keep to yourself; whereby you will know that I have always had my eye on you. Suppose that at this moment some God came to you and said: Alcibiades, will you live as you are, or die in an instant if you are forbidden to make any further acquisition? - I verily believe that you would choose death. And I will tell you the hope in which you are at present living: Before many days have elapsed, you think that you will come before the Athenian assembly, and will prove to them that you are more worthy of honour than Pericles, or any other man that ever lived, and having proved this, you will have the greatest power in the state. When you have gained the greatest power among us, you will go on to other Hellenic states, and not only to Hellenes, but to all the barbarians who inhabit the same continent with us. And if the God were then to say to you again: Here in Europe is to be your seat of empire, and you must not cross over into Asia or meddle with Asiatic affairs, I do not believe that you would choose to live upon these terms; but the world, as I may say, must be filled with your power and name - no man less than Cyrus and Xerxes is of any account with you. Such I know to be your hopes - I am not guessing only - and very likely you, who know that I am speaking the truth, will reply, Well, Socrates, but what have my hopes to do with the explanation which you promised of your unwillingness to leave me? And that is what I am now going to tell you, sweet son of Cleinias and Dinomache. The explanation is, that all these designs of yours cannot be accomplished by you without my help; so great is the power which I believe myself to have over you and your concerns; and this I conceive to be the reason why the God has hitherto forbidden me to converse with you, and I have been long expecting his permission. For, as you hope to prove your own great value to the state, and having proved it, to attain at once to absolute power, so do I indulge a hope that I shall be the supreme power over you, if I am able to prove my own great value to you, and to show you that neither guardian, nor kinsman, nor any one is able to deliver into your hands the power which you desire, but I only, God being my helper. When you were young (compare Symp.) and your hopes were not yet matured, I should have wasted my time, and therefore, as I conceive, the God forbade me to converse with you; but now, having his permission, I will speak, for now you will listen to me.

ALCIBIADES: Your silence, Socrates, was

always a surprise to me. I never could understand why you followed me about, and now that you have begun to speak again, I am still more amazed. Whether I think all this or not, is a matter about which you seem to have already made up your mind, and therefore my denial will have no effect upon you. But granting, if I must, that you have perfectly divined my purposes, why is your assistance necessary to the attainment of them? Can you tell me why?

SOCRATES: You want to know whether I can make a long speech, such as you are in the habit of hearing; but that is not my way. I think, however, that I can prove to you the truth of what I am saying, if you will grant me one little favour.

ALCIBIADES: Yes, if the favour which you mean be not a troublesome one.

SOCRATES: Will you be troubled at having questions to answer?

ALCIBIADES: Not at all.

SOCRATES: Then please to answer.

ALCIBIADES: Ask me.

SOCRATES: Have you not the intention which I attribute to you?

ALCIBIADES: I will grant anything you like, in the hope of hearing what more you have to say.

SOCRATES: You do, then, mean, as I was saying, to come forward in a little while in the character of an adviser of the Athenians? And suppose that when you are ascending the bema, I pull you by the sleeve and say, Alcibiades, you are getting up to advise the Athenians - do you know the matter about which they are going to deliberate, better than they?—How would you answer?

ALCIBIADES: I should reply, that I was going to advise them about a matter which I do know better than they.

SOCRATES: Then you are a good adviser about the things which you know?

ALCIBIADES: Certainly.

SOCRATES: And do you know anything but what you have learned of others, or found out yourself?

ALCIBIADES: That is all.

SOCRATES: And would you have ever learned or discovered anything, if you had not been willing either to learn of others or to examine yourself?

ALCIBIADES: I should not.

SOCRATES: And would you have been willing to learn or to examine what you supposed that you knew?

ALCIBIADES: Certainly not.

SOCRATES: Then there was a time when you thought that you did not know what you are now supposed to know?

ALCIBIADES: Certainly.

SOCRATES: I think that I know tolerably well the extent of your acquirements; and you must tell me if I forget any of them: according to my recollection, you learned the arts of writing, of playing on the lyre, and of wrestling; the flute you never would learn; this is the sum of your accomplishments, unless there were some which you acquired in secret; and I think that secrecy was hardly possible, as you could not have come out of your door, either by day or night, without my seeing you.

ALCIBIADES: Yes, that was the whole of my schooling.

SOCRATES: And are you going to get up in the Athenian assembly, and give them advice about writing?

ALCIBIADES: No, indeed.

SOCRATES: Or about the touch of the lyre?

ALCIBIADES: Certainly not.

SOCRATES: And they are not in the habit of deliberating about wrestling, in the assembly?

ALCIBIADES: Hardly.

SOCRATES: Then what are the deliberations in which you propose to advise them? Surely not about building?

ALCIBIADES: No.

SOCRATES: For the builder will advise better than you will about that?

ALCIBIADES: He will.

SOCRATES: Nor about divination?

ALCIBIADES: No.

SOCRATES: About that again the diviner will advise better than you will?

ALCIBIADES: True.

SOCRATES: Whether he be little or great, good or ill-looking, noble or ignoble - makes no difference.

ALCIBIADES: Certainly not.

SOCRATES: A man is a good adviser about anything, not because he has riches, but because he has knowledge?

ALCIBIADES: Assuredly.

SOCRATES: Whether their counsellor is rich or poor, is not a matter which will make any difference to the Athenians when they are deliberating about the health of the citizens; they only require that he should be a physician.

ALCIBIADES: Of course.

SOCRATES: Then what will be the subject of deliberation about which you will be justified in getting up and advising them?

ALCIBIADES: About their own concerns, Socrates.

SOCRATES: You mean about shipbuilding, for example, when the question is what sort of ships they ought to build?

ALCIBIADES: No, I should not advise them about that.

SOCRATES: I suppose, because you do not understand shipbuilding: - is that the reason?

ALCIBIADES: It is.

SOCRATES: Then about what concerns of theirs will you advise them?

ALCIBIADES: About war, Socrates, or about peace, or about any other concerns of the state.

SOCRATES: You mean, when they deliberate with whom they ought to make peace, and with whom they ought to go to war, and in what manner?

ALCIBIADES: Yes.

SOCRATES: And they ought to go to war

with those against whom it is better to go to war?

ALCIBIADES: Yes.

SOCRATES: And when it is better?

ALCIBIADES: Certainly.

SOCRATES: And for as long a time as is better?

ALCIBIADES: Yes.

SOCRATES: But suppose the Athenians to deliberate with whom they ought to close in wrestling, and whom they should grasp by the hand, would you, or the master of gymnastics, be a better adviser of them?

ALCIBIADES: Clearly, the master of gymnastics.

SOCRATES: And can you tell me on what grounds the master of gymnastics would decide, with whom they ought or ought not to close, and when and how? To take an instance: Would he not say that they should wrestle with those against whom it is best to wrestle?

ALCIBIADES: Yes.

SOCRATES: And as much as is best?

ALCIBIADES: Certainly.

SOCRATES: And at such times as are best?

ALCIBIADES: Yes.

SOCRATES: Again; you sometimes accompany the lyre with the song and dance?

ALCIBIADES: Yes.

SOCRATES: When it is well to do so?

ALCIBIADES: Yes.

SOCRATES: And as much as is well?

ALCIBIADES: Just so.

SOCRATES: And as you speak of an excellence or art of the best in wrestling, and of an excellence in playing the lyre, I wish you would tell me what this latter is; - the excellence of wrestling I call gymnastic, and I want to know what you call the other.

ALCIBIADES: I do not understand you.

SOCRATES: Then try to do as I do; for the answer which I gave is universally right, and when I say right, I mean according to rule.

ALCIBIADES: Yes.

SOCRATES: And was not the art of which I spoke gymnastic?

ALCIBIADES: Certainly.

SOCRATES: And I called the excellence in wrestling gymnastic?

ALCIBIADES: You did.

SOCRATES: And I was right?

ALCIBIADES: I think that you were.

SOCRATES: Well, now, - for you should learn to argue prettily - let me ask you in return to tell me, first, what is that art of which playing and singing, and stepping properly in the dance, are parts, - what is the name of the whole? I think that by this time you must be able to tell.

ALCIBIADES: Indeed I cannot.

SOCRATES: Then let me put the matter in

another way: what do you call the Goddesses who are the patronesses of art?

ALCIBIADES: The Muses do you mean, Socrates?

SOCRATES: Yes, I do; and what is the name of the art which is called after them?

ALCIBIADES: I suppose that you mean music.

SOCRATES: Yes, that is my meaning; and what is the excellence of the art of music, as I told you truly that the excellence of wrestling was gymnastic - what is the excellence of music - to be what?

ALCIBIADES: To be musical, I suppose.

SOCRATES: Very good; and now please to tell me what is the excellence of war and peace; as the more musical was the more excellent, or the more gymnastical was the more excellent, tell me, what name do you give to the more excellent in war and peace?

ALCIBIADES: But I really cannot tell you.

SOCRATES: But if you were offering advice to another and said to him—This food is better than that, at this time and in this quantity, and he said to you--What do you mean, Alcibiades, by the word 'better'? you would have no difficulty in replying that you meant 'more wholesome,' although you do not profess to be a physician: and when the subject is one of which you profess to have knowledge, and about which you are ready to get up and advise as if you knew, are you not ashamed, when you are asked, not to be able to answer the question? Is it not disgraceful?

ALCIBIADES: Very.

SOCRATES: Well, then, consider and try to explain what is the meaning of 'better,' in the matter of making peace and going to war with those against whom you ought to go to war? To what does the word refer?

ALCIBIADES: I am thinking, and I cannot tell.

SOCRATES: But you surely know what are the charges which we bring against one another, when we arrive at the point of making war, and what name we give them?

ALCIBIADES: Yes, certainly; we say that deceit or violence has been employed, or that we have been defrauded.

SOCRATES: And how does this happen? Will you tell me how? For there may be a difference in the manner.

ALCIBIADES: Do you mean by 'how,' Socrates, whether we suffered these things justly or unjustly?

SOCRATES: Exactly.

ALCIBIADES: There can be no greater difference than between just and unjust.

SOCRATES: And would you advise the Athenians to go to war with the just or with the unjust?

ALCIBIADES: That is an awkward question; for certainly, even if a person did intend to go to war with the just, he would not admit that they were just.

SOCRATES: He would not go to war, because it would be unlawful?

ALCIBIADES: Neither lawful nor honourable.

SOCRATES: Then you, too, would address them on principles of justice?

ALCIBIADES: Certainly.

SOCRATES: What, then, is justice but that better, of which I spoke, in going to war or not going to war with those against whom we ought or ought not, and when we ought or ought not to go to war?

ALCIBIADES: Clearly.

SOCRATES: But how is this, friend Alcibiades? Have you forgotten that you do not know this, or have you been to the schoolmaster without my knowledge, and has he taught you to discern the just from the unjust? Who is he? I wish you would tell me, that I may go and learn of him - you shall introduce me.

ALCIBIADES: You are mocking, Socrates.

SOCRATES: No, indeed; I most solemnly declare to you by Zeus, who is the God of our common friendship, and whom I never will forswear, that I am not; tell me, then, who this instructor is, if he exists.

ALCIBIADES: But, perhaps, he does not exist; may I not have acquired the knowledge of just and unjust in some other way?

SOCRATES: Yes; if you have discovered them.

ALCIBIADES: But do you not think that I could discover them?

SOCRATES: I am sure that you might, if you enquired about them.

ALCIBIADES: And do you not think that I would enquire?

SOCRATES: Yes; if you thought that you did not know them.

ALCIBIADES: And was there not a time when I did so think?

SOCRATES: Very good; and can you tell me how long it is since you thought that you did not know the nature of the just and the unjust? What do you say to a year ago? Were you then in a state of conscious ignorance and enquiry? Or did you think that you knew? And please to answer truly, that our discussion may not be in vain.

ALCIBIADES: Well, I thought that I knew.

SOCRATES: And two years ago, and three

years ago, and four years ago, you knew all the same?

ALCIBIADES: I did.

SOCRATES: And more than four years ago you were a child - were you not?

ALCIBIADES: Yes.

SOCRATES: And then I am quite sure that you thought you knew.

ALCIBIADES: Why are you so sure?

SOCRATES: Because I often heard you when a child, in your teacher's house, or elsewhere, playing at dice or some other game with the boys, not hesitating at all about the nature of the just and unjust; but very confident - crying and shouting that one of the boys was a rogue and a cheat, and had been cheating. Is it not true?

ALCIBIADES: But what was I to do, Socrates, when anybody cheated me?

SOCRATES: And how can you say, 'What was I to do'? if at the time you did not know whether you were wronged or not?

ALCIBIADES: To be sure I knew; I was quite aware that I was being cheated.

SOCRATES: Then you suppose yourself even when a child to have known the nature of just and unjust?

ALCIBIADES: Certainly; and I did know then.

SOCRATES: And when did you discover them - not, surely, at the time when you thought that you knew them?

ALCIBIADES: Certainly not.

SOCRATES: And when did you think that you were ignorant - if you consider, you will find that there never was such a time?

ALCIBIADES: Really, Socrates, I cannot say.

SOCRATES: Then you did not learn them by discovering them?

ALCIBIADES: Clearly not.

SOCRATES: But just before you said that you did not know them by learning; now, if you have neither discovered nor learned them, how and whence do you come to know them?

ALCIBIADES: I suppose that I was mistaken in saying that I knew them through my own discovery of them; whereas, in truth, I learned them in the same way that other people learn.

SOCRATES: So you said before, and I must again ask, of whom? Do tell me.

ALCIBIADES: Of the many.

SOCRATES: Do you take refuge in them? I cannot say much for your teachers.

ALCIBIADES: Why, are they not able to teach?

SOCRATES: They could not teach you how to play at draughts, which you would acknowledge (would you not) to be a much smaller matter than justice?

ALCIBIADES: Yes.

SOCRATES: And can they teach the better who are unable to teach the worse?

ALCIBIADES: I think that they can; at any rate, they can teach many far better things than to play at draughts.

SOCRATES: What things?

ALCIBIADES: Why, for example, I learned to speak Greek of them, and I cannot say who was my teacher, or to whom I am to attribute my knowledge of Greek, if not to those good-for-nothing teachers, as you call them.

SOCRATES: Why, yes, my friend; and the many are good enough teachers of Greek, and some of their instructions in that line may be justly praised.

ALCIBIADES: Why is that?

SOCRATES: Why, because they have the qualities which good teachers ought to have.

ALCIBIADES: What qualities?

SOCRATES: Why, you know that knowledge is the first qualification of any teacher?

ALCIBIADES: Certainly.

SOCRATES: And if they know, they must agree together and not differ?

ALCIBIADES: Yes.

SOCRATES: And would you say that they knew the things about which they differ?

ALCIBIADES: No.

SOCRATES: Then how can they teach them?

ALCIBIADES: They cannot.

SOCRATES: Well, but do you imagine that the many would differ about the nature of wood and stone? are they not agreed if you ask them what they are? and do they not run to fetch the same thing, when they want a piece of wood or a stone? And so in similar cases, which I suspect to be pretty nearly all that you mean by speaking Greek.

ALCIBIADES: True.

SOCRATES: These, as we were saying, are matters about which they are agreed with one another and with themselves; both individuals and states use the same words about them; they do not use some one word and some another.

ALCIBIADES: They do not.

SOCRATES: Then they may be expected to be good teachers of these things?

ALCIBIADES: Yes.

SOCRATES: And if we want to instruct any one in them, we shall be right in sending him to be taught by our friends the many?

ALCIBIADES: Very true.

SOCRATES: But if we wanted further to know not only which are men and which are horses, but which men or horses have powers of running, would the many still be able to inform us?

ALCIBIADES: Certainly not.

SOCRATES: And you have a sufficient proof that they do not know these things and are not the best teachers of them, inasmuch as they are never agreed about them?

ALCIBIADES: Yes.

SOCRATES: And suppose that we wanted to know not only what men are like, but what healthy or diseased men are like - would the many be able to teach us?

ALCIBIADES: They would not.

SOCRATES: And you would have a proof that they were bad teachers of these matters, if you saw them at variance?

ALCIBIADES: I should.

SOCRATES: Well, but are the many agreed with themselves, or with one another, about the justice or injustice of men and things?

ALCIBIADES: Assuredly not, Socrates.

SOCRATES: There is no subject about which they are more at variance?

ALCIBIADES: None.

SOCRATES: I do not suppose that you ever saw or heard of men quarrelling over the principles of health and disease to such an extent as to go to war and kill one another for the sake of them?

ALCIBIADES: No indeed.

SOCRATES: But of the quarrels about justice and injustice, even if you have never seen them, you have certainly heard from many people, including Homer; for you have heard of the Iliad and Odyssey?

ALCIBIADES: To be sure, Socrates.

SOCRATES: A difference of just and unjust is the argument of those poems?

ALCIBIADES: True.

SOCRATES: Which difference caused all the wars and deaths of Trojans and Achaeans, and the deaths of the suitors of Penelope in their quarrel with Odysseus.

ALCIBIADES: Very true.

SOCRATES: And when the Athenians and Lacedaemonians and Boeotians fell at Tanagra, and afterwards in the battle of Coronea, at which your father Cleinias met his end, the question was one of justice - this was the sole cause of the battles, and of their deaths.

ALCIBIADES: Very true.

SOCRATES: But can they be said to under-stand that about which they are quarrelling to the death?

ALCIBIADES: Clearly not.

SOCRATES: And yet those whom you thus allow to be ignorant are the teachers to whom you are appealing.

ALCIBIADES: Very true.

SOCRATES: But how are you ever likely to know the nature of justice and injustice, about which you are so perplexed, if you have neither learned them of others nor discovered them yourself?

ALCIBIADES: From what you say, I suppose not.

SOCRATES: See, again, how inaccurately you speak, Alcibiades!

ALCIBIADES: In what respect?

SOCRATES: In saying that I say so.

ALCIBIADES: Why, did you not say that I know nothing of the just and unjust?

SOCRATES: No; I did not.

ALCIBIADES: Did I, then?

SOCRATES: Yes.

ALCIBIADES: How was that?

SOCRATES: Let me explain. Suppose I were to ask you which is the greater number, two or one; you would reply 'two'?

ALCIBIADES: I should.

SOCRATES: And by how much greater?

ALCIBIADES: By one.

SOCRATES: Which of us now says that two is more than one?

ALCIBIADES: I do.

SOCRATES: Did not I ask, and you answer the question?

ALCIBIADES: Yes.

SOCRATES: Then who is speaking? I who put the question, or you who answer me?

ALCIBIADES: I am.

SOCRATES: Or suppose that I ask and you tell me the letters which make up the name Socrates, which of us is the speaker?

ALCIBIADES: I am.

SOCRATES: Now let us put the case generally: whenever there is a question and answer, who is the speaker, - the questioner or the answerer?

ALCIBIADES: I should say, Socrates, that the answerer was the speaker.

SOCRATES: And have I not been the questioner all through?

ALCIBIADES: Yes.

SOCRATES: And you the answerer?

ALCIBIADES: Just so.

SOCRATES: Which of us, then, was the speaker?

ALCIBIADES: The inference is, Socrates, that I was the speaker.

SOCRATES: Did not some one say that Alcibiades, the fair son of Cleinias, not under-standing about just and unjust, but thinking that he did understand, was going to the assembly to advise the Athenians about what he did not know? Was not that said?

ALCIBIADES: Very true.

SOCRATES: Then, Alcibiades, the result may be expressed in the language of Euripides. I think that you have heard all this 'from yourself, and not from me'; nor did I say this, which you erroneously attribute to me, but you yourself, and what you said was very true. For indeed, my dear fellow, the design which you meditate of teaching what you do not know, and have not taken any pains to learn, is downright insanity.

ALCIBIADES: But, Socrates, I think that the Athenians and the rest of the Hellenes do not often advise as to the more just or unjust; for they see no difficulty in them, and therefore they leave them, and consider which course of action will be most expedient; for there is a difference between justice and expediency. Many persons have done great wrong and profited by their injustice; others have done rightly and come to no good.

SOCRATES: Well, but granting that the just and the expedient are ever so much opposed, you surely do not imagine that you know what is expedient for mankind, or why a thing is expedient?

ALCIBIADES: Why not, Socrates? - But I am not going to be asked again from whom I learned, or when I made the discovery.

SOCRATES: What a way you have! When you make a mistake which might be refuted by a previous argument, you insist on having a new and different refutation; the old argument is a worn-our garment which you will no longer put on, but some one must produce another which is clean and new. Now I shall disregard this move of yours, and shall ask over again, - Where did you learn and how do you know the nature of the expedient, and who is your teacher? All this I comprehend in a single question, and now you will manifestly be in the old difficulty, and will not be able to show that you know the expedient, either because you learned or because you discovered it yourself. But, as I perceive that you are dainty, and dislike the taste of a stale argument, I will enquire no further into your knowledge of what is expedient or what is not expedient for the Athenian people, and simply request you to say why you do not explain whether justice and expediency are the same or different? And if you like you may examine me as I have examined you, or, if you would rather, you may carry on the discussion by yourself.

ALCIBIADES: But I am not certain, Socrates, whether I shall be able to discuss the matter with you.

SOCRATES: Then imagine, my dear fellow, that I am the demus and the ecclesia; for in the ecclesia, too, you will have to persuade men individually.

ALCIBIADES: Yes.

SOCRATES: And is not the same person able to persuade one individual singly and many individuals of the things which he knows? The grammarian, for example, can persuade one and he can persuade many about letters.

ALCIBIADES: True.

SOCRATES: And about number, will not the same person persuade one and persuade many?

ALCIBIADES: Yes.

SOCRATES: And this will be he who knows number, or the arithmetician?

ALCIBIADES: Quite true.

SOCRATES: And cannot you persuade one man about that of which you can persuade many?

ALCIBIADES: I suppose so.

SOCRATES: And that of which you can persuade either is clearly what you know?

ALCIBIADES: Yes.

SOCRATES: And the only difference between one who argues as we are doing, and the orator who is addressing an assembly, is that the one seeks to persuade a number, and the other an individual, of the same things.

ALCIBIADES: I suppose so.

SOCRATES: Well, then, since the same person who can persuade a multitude can persuade individuals, try conclusions upon me, and prove to me that the just is not always expedient.

ALCIBIADES: You take liberties, Socrates.

SOCRATES: I shall take the liberty of proving to you the opposite of that which you will not prove to me.

ALCIBIADES: Proceed.

SOCRATES: Answer my questions - that is all.

ALCIBIADES: Nay, I should like you to be the speaker.

SOCRATES: What, do you not wish to be persuaded?

ALCIBIADES: Certainly I do.

SOCRATES: And can you be persuaded better than out of your own mouth?

ALCIBIADES: I think not.

SOCRATES: Then you shall answer; and if you do not hear the words, that the just is the expedient, coming from your own lips, never believe another man again.

ALCIBIADES: I won't; but answer I will, for I do not see how I can come to any harm.

SOCRATES: A true prophecy! Let me begin then by enquiring of you whether you allow that the just is sometimes expedient and sometimes not?

ALCIBIADES: Yes.

SOCRATES: And sometimes honourable and sometimes not?

ALCIBIADES: What do you mean?

SOCRATES: I am asking if you ever knew any one who did what was dishonourable and yet just?

ALCIBIADES: Never.

SOCRATES: All just things are honourable?

ALCIBIADES: Yes.

SOCRATES: And are honourable things sometimes good and sometimes not good, or are they always good?

ALCIBIADES: I rather think, Socrates, that some honourable things are evil.

SOCRATES: And are some dishonourable things good?

ALCIBIADES: Yes.

SOCRATES: You mean in such a case as the following: - In time of war, men have been wounded or have died in rescuing a companion or kinsman, when others who have neglected the duty of rescuing them have escaped in safety?

ALCIBIADES: True.

SOCRATES: And to rescue another under such circumstances is honourable, in respect of the attempt to save those whom we ought to save; and this is courage?

ALCIBIADES: True.

SOCRATES: But evil in respect of death and wounds?

ALCIBIADES: Yes.

SOCRATES: And the courage which is shown in the rescue is one thing, and the death another?

ALCIBIADES: Certainly.

SOCRATES: Then the rescue of one's friends is honourable in one point of view, but evil in another?

ALCIBIADES: True.

SOCRATES: And if honourable, then also good: Will you consider now whether I may not be right, for you were acknowledging that the courage which is shown in the rescue is honourable? Now is this courage good or evil? Look at the matter thus: which would you rather choose, good or evil?

ALCIBIADES: Good.

SOCRATES: And the greatest goods you would be most ready to choose, and would least like to be deprived of them?

ALCIBIADES: Certainly.

SOCRATES: What would you say of courage? At what price would you be willing to be deprived of courage?

ALCIBIADES: I would rather die than be a coward.

SOCRATES: Then you think that cowardice is the worst of evils?

ALCIBIADES: I do.

SOCRATES: As bad as death, I suppose?

ALCIBIADES: Yes.

SOCRATES: And life and courage are the extreme opposites of death and cowardice?

ALCIBIADES: Yes.

SOCRATES: And they are what you would most desire to have, and their opposites you would least desire?

ALCIBIADES: Yes.

SOCRATES: Is this because you think life and courage the best, and death and cowardice the worst?

ALCIBIADES: Yes.

SOCRATES: And you would term the rescue of a friend in battle honourable, in as much as courage does a good work?

ALCIBIADES: I should.

SOCRATES: But evil because of the death which ensues?

ALCIBIADES: Yes.

SOCRATES: Might we not describe their different effects as follows: - You may call either of them evil in respect of the evil which is the result, and good in respect of the good which is the result of either of them?

ALCIBIADES: Yes.

SOCRATES: And they are honourable in so far as they are good, and dishonourable in so far as they are evil?

ALCIBIADES: True.

SOCRATES: Then when you say that the rescue of a friend in battle is honourable and yet evil, that is equivalent to saying that the rescue is good and yet evil?

ALCIBIADES: I believe that you are right, Socrates.

SOCRATES: Nothing honourable, regarded as honourable, is evil; nor anything base, regarded as base, good.

ALCIBIADES: Clearly not.

SOCRATES: Look at the matter yet once more in a further light: he who acts honourably acts well?

ALCIBIADES: Yes.

SOCRATES: And he who acts well is happy?

ALCIBIADES: Of course.

SOCRATES: And the happy are those who obtain good?

ALCIBIADES: True.

SOCRATES: And they obtain good by acting well and honourably?

ALCIBIADES: Yes.

SOCRATES: Then acting well is a good?

ALCIBIADES: Certainly.

SOCRATES: And happiness is a good?

ALCIBIADES: Yes.

SOCRATES: Then the good and the honourable are again identified.

ALCIBIADES: Manifestly.

SOCRATES: Then, if the argument holds, what we find to be honourable we shall also find to be good?

ALCIBIADES: Certainly.

SOCRATES: And is the good expedient or not?

ALCIBIADES: Expedient.

SOCRATES: Do you remember our admissions about the just?

ALCIBIADES: Yes; if I am not mistaken, we said that those who acted justly must also act honourably.

SOCRATES: And the honourable is the good?

ALCIBIADES: Yes.

SOCRATES: And the good is expedient?

ALCIBIADES: Yes.

SOCRATES: Then, Alcibiades, the just is expedient?

ALCIBIADES: I should infer so.

SOCRATES: And all this I prove out of your own mouth, for I ask and you answer?

ALCIBIADES: I must acknowledge it to be true.

SOCRATES: And having acknowledged that the just is the same as the expedient, are you not (let me ask) prepared to ridicule any one who, pretending to understand the principles of justice and injustice, gets up to advise the noble Athenians or the ignoble Peparethians, that the just may be the evil?

ALCIBIADES: I solemnly declare, Socrates, that I do not know what I am saying. Verily, I am in a strange state, for when you put questions to me I am of different minds in successive instants.

SOCRATES: And are you not aware of the nature of this perplexity, my friend?

ALCIBIADES: Indeed I am not.

SOCRATES: Do you suppose that if some one were to ask you whether you have two eyes or three, or two hands or four, or anything of that sort, you would then be of different minds in successive instants?

ALCIBIADES: I begin to distrust myself, but still I do not suppose that I should.

SOCRATES: You would feel no doubt; and for this reason - because you would know?

ALCIBIADES: I suppose so.

SOCRATES: And the reason why you involuntarily contradict yourself is clearly that you are ignorant?

ALCIBIADES: Very likely.

SOCRATES: And if you are perplexed in answering about just and unjust, honourable and dishonourable, good and evil, expedient and inexpedient, the reason is that you are ignorant of them, and therefore in perplexity. Is not that clear?

ALCIBIADES: I agree.

SOCRATES: But is this always the case, and is a man necessarily perplexed about that of which he has no knowledge?

ALCIBIADES: Certainly he is.

SOCRATES: And do you know how to ascend into heaven?

ALCIBIADES: Certainly not.

SOCRATES: And in this case, too, is your judgment perplexed?

ALCIBIADES: No.

SOCRATES: Do you see the reason why, or shall I tell you?

ALCIBIADES: Tell me.

SOCRATES: The reason is, that you not only do not know, my friend, but you do not think that you know.

ALCIBIADES: There again; what do you mean?

SOCRATES: Ask yourself; are you in any perplexity about things of which you are ignorant? You know, for example, that you know nothing about the preparation of food.

ALCIBIADES: Very true.

SOCRATES: And do you think and perplex yourself about the preparation of food: or do you leave that to some one who understands the art?

ALCIBIADES: The latter.

SOCRATES: Or if you were on a voyage, would you bewilder yourself by considering whether the rudder is to be drawn inwards or outwards, or do you leave that to the pilot, and do nothing?

ALCIBIADES: It would be the concern of the pilot.

SOCRATES: Then you are not perplexed about what you do not know, if you know that you do not know it?

ALCIBIADES: I imagine not.

SOCRATES: Do you not see, then, that mistakes in life and practice are likewise to be attributed to the ignorance which has conceit of knowledge?

ALCIBIADES: Once more, what do you mean?

SOCRATES: I suppose that we begin to act when we think that we know what we are doing?

ALCIBIADES: Yes.

SOCRATES: But when people think that they do not know, they entrust their business to others?

ALCIBIADES: Yes.

SOCRATES: And so there is a class of ignorant persons who do not make mistakes in life, because they trust others about things of which they are ignorant?

ALCIBIADES: True.

SOCRATES: Who, then, are the persons who make mistakes? They cannot, of course, be those who know?

ALCIBIADES: Certainly not.

SOCRATES: But if neither those who know, nor those who know that they do not know, make mistakes, there remain those only who do not know and think that they know.

ALCIBIADES: Yes, only those.

SOCRATES: Then this is ignorance of the disgraceful sort which is mischievous?

ALCIBIADES: Yes.

SOCRATES: And most mischievous and most disgraceful when having to do with the greatest matters?

ALCIBIADES: By far.

SOCRATES: And can there be any matters

greater than the just, the honourable, the good, and the expedient?

ALCIBIADES: There cannot be.

SOCRATES: And these, as you were saying, are what perplex you?

ALCIBIADES: Yes.

SOCRATES: But if you are perplexed, then, as the previous argument has shown, you are not only ignorant of the greatest matters, but being ignorant you fancy that you know them?

ALCIBIADES: I fear that you are right.

SOCRATES: And now see what has happened to you, Alcibiades! I hardly like to speak of your evil case, but as we are alone I will: My good friend, you are wedded to ignorance of the most disgraceful kind, and of this you are convicted, not by me, but out of your own mouth and by your own argument; wherefore also you rush into politics before you are educated. Neither is your case to be deemed singular. For I might say the same of almost all our statesmen, with the exception, perhaps of your guardian, Pericles.

ALCIBIADES: Yes, Socrates; and Pericles is said not to have got his wisdom by the light of nature, but to have associated with several of the philosophers; with Pythocleides, for example, and with Anaxagoras, and now in advanced life with Damon, in the hope of gaining wisdom.

SOCRATES: Very good; but did you ever know a man wise in anything who was unable to impart his particular wisdom? For example, he who taught you letters was not only wise, but he made you and any others whom he liked wise.

ALCIBIADES: Yes.

SOCRATES: And you, whom he taught, can do the same?

ALCIBIADES: True.

SOCRATES: And in like manner the harper and gymnastic-master?

ALCIBIADES: Certainly.

SOCRATES: When a person is enabled to impart knowledge to another, he thereby gives an excellent proof of his own understanding of any matter.

ALCIBIADES: I agree.

SOCRATES: Well, and did Pericles make any one wise; did he begin by making his sons wise?

ALCIBIADES: But, Socrates, if the two sons of Pericles were simpletons, what has that to do with the matter?

SOCRATES: Well, but did he make your brother, Cleinias, wise?

ALCIBIADES: Cleinias is a madman; there is no use in talking of him.

SOCRATES: But if Cleinias is a madman and the two sons of Pericles were simpletons, what reason can be given why he neglects you, and lets you be as you are?

ALCIBIADES: I believe that I am to blame for not listening to him.

SOCRATES: But did you ever hear of any other Athenian or foreigner, bond or free, who was deemed to have grown wiser in the society of Pericles, - as I might cite Pythodorus, the son of Isolochus, and Callias, the son of Calliades, who have grown wiser in the society of Zeno, for which privilege they have each of them paid him the sum of a hundred minae (about 406 pounds sterling) to the increase of their wisdom and fame.

ALCIBIADES: I certainly never did hear of any one.

SOCRATES: Well, and in reference to your own case, do you mean to remain as you are, or will you take some pains about yourself?

ALCIBIADES: With your aid, Socrates, I will. And indeed, when I hear you speak, the truth of what you are saying strikes home to me, and I agree with you, for our states-men, all but a few, do appear to be quite uneducated.

SOCRATES: What is the inference?

ALCIBIADES: Why, that if they were educated they would be trained athletes, and he who means to rival them ought to have knowledge and experience when he attacks them; but now, as they have become politicians without any special training, why should I have the trouble of learning and practising? For I know well that by the light of nature I shall get the better of them.

SOCRATES: My dear friend, what a

sentiment! And how unworthy of your noble form and your high estate!

ALCIBIADES: What do you mean, Socrates; why do you say so?

SOCRATES: I am grieved when I think of our mutual love.

ALCIBIADES: At what?

SOCRATES: At your fancying that the contest on which you are entering is with people here.

ALCIBIADES: Why, what others are there?

SOCRATES: Is that a question which a magnanimous soul should ask?

ALCIBIADES: Do you mean to say that the contest is not with these?

SOCRATES: And suppose that you were going to steer a ship into action, would you only aim at being the best pilot on board? Would you not, while acknowledging that you must possess this degree of excellence, rather look to your antagonists, and not, as you are now doing, to your fellow combatants? You ought to be so far above these latter, that they will not even dare to be your rivals; and, being regarded by you as inferiors, will do battle for you against the enemy; this is the kind of superiority which you must establish over them, if you mean to accomplish any noble action really worthy of yourself and of the state.

ALCIBIADES: That would certainly be my aim.

SOCRATES: Verily, then, you have good reason to be satisfied, if you are better than the soldiers; and you need not, when you are their superior and have your thoughts and actions fixed upon them, look away to the generals of the enemy.

ALCIBIADES: Of whom are you speaking, Socrates?

SOCRATES: Why, you surely know that our city goes to war now and then with the Lacedaemonians and with the great king?

ALCIBIADES: True enough.

SOCRATES: And if you meant to be the ruler of this city, would you not be right in considering that the Lacedaemonian and Persian king were your true rivals?

ALCIBIADES: I believe that you are right.

SOCRATES: Oh no, my friend, I am quite wrong, and I think that you ought rather to turn your attention to Midias the quail-breeder and others like him, who manage our politics; in whom, as the women would remark, you may still see the slaves' cut of hair, cropping out in their minds as well as on their pates; and they come with their barbarous lingo to flatter us and not to rule us. To these, I say, you should look, and then you need not trouble yourself about your own fitness to contend in such a noble arena: there is no reason why you should either learn what has to be learned, or practise what has to be practised, and only when thoroughly prepared enter on a political career.

ALCIBIADES: There, I think, Socrates, that you are right; I do not suppose, however, that the Spartan generals or the great king are really different from anybody else.

SOCRATES: But, my dear friend, do consider what you are saying.

ALCIBIADES: What am I to consider?

SOCRATES: In the first place, will you be more likely to take care of yourself, if you are in a wholesome fear and dread of them, or if you are not?

ALCIBIADES: Clearly, if I have such a fear of them.

SOCRATES: And do you think that you will sustain any injury if you take care of yourself?

ALCIBIADES: No, I shall be greatly benefited.

SOCRATES: And this is one very important respect in which that notion of yours is bad.

ALCIBIADES: True.

SOCRATES: In the next place, consider that what you say is probably false.

ALCIBIADES: How so?

SOCRATES: Let me ask you whether better natures are likely to be found in noble races or not in noble races?

ALCIBIADES: Clearly in noble races.

SOCRATES: Are not those who are well born

and well bred most likely to be perfect in virtue?

ALCIBIADES: Certainly.

SOCRATES: Then let us compare our antecedents with those of the Lacedaemonian and Persian kings; are they inferior to us in descent? Have we not heard that the former are sprung from Heracles, and the latter from Achaemenes, and that the race of Heracles and the race of Achaemenes go back to Perseus, son of Zeus?

ALCIBIADES: Why, so does mine go back to Eurysaces, and he to Zeus!

SOCRATES: And mine, noble Alcibiades, to Daedalus, and he to Hephaestus, son of Zeus. But, for all that, we are far inferior to them. For they are descended 'from Zeus,' through a line of kings - either kings of Argos and Lacedaemon, or kings of Persia, a country which the descendants of Achaemenes have always possessed, besides being at various times sovereigns of Asia, as they now are; whereas, we and our fathers were but private persons. How ridiculous would you be thought if you were to make a display of your ancestors and of Salamis the island of Eurysaces, or of Aegina, the habitation of the still more ancient Aeacus, before Artaxerxes, son of Xerxes. You should consider how inferior we are to them both in the derivation of our birth and in other particulars. Did you never observe how great is the property of the Spartan kings? And their wives are under the guardianship of the Ephori, who are public officers and watch over them, in order to preserve as far as possible the purity of the Heracleid blood. Still greater is the difference among the Persians; for no one entertains a suspicion that the father of a prince of Persia can be any one but the king. Such is the awe which invests the person of the queen, that any other guard is needless. And when the heir of the kingdom is born, all the subjects of the king feast; and the day of his birth is for ever afterwards kept as a holiday and time of sacrifice by all Asia; whereas, when you and I were born, Alcibiades, as the comic poet says, the neighbours hardly knew of the important event. After the birth of the royal child, he is tended, not by a good-for-nothing woman-nurse, but by the best of the royal eunuchs, who are charged with the care of him, and especially with the fashioning and right formation of his limbs, in order that he may be as shapely as possible; which being their calling, they are held in great honour. And when the young prince is seven years old he is put upon a horse and taken to the riding masters, and begins to go out hunting. And at fourteen years of age he is handed over to the royal schoolmasters, as they are termed: these are four chosen men, reputed to be the best among the Persians of a certain age; and one of them is the wisest, another the justest, a third the most temperate, and a fourth the most valiant. The first instructs him in the magianism of Zoroaster, the son of Oromasus, which is the worship of the Gods, and teaches him also the duties of his royal office; the second, who is the justest, teaches him always to speak the truth; the third, or most temperate, forbids him to allow any pleasure to be lord over him, that he may be accustomed to be a freeman and king indeed, - lord of himself first, and not a slave; the most valiant trains him to be bold and fearless, telling him that if he fears he is to deem himself a slave; whereas Pericles gave you, Alcibiades, for a tutor Zopyrus the Thracian, a slave of his who was past all other work. I might enlarge on the nurture and education of your rivals, but that would be tedious; and what I have said is a sufficient sample of what remains to be said. I have only to remark, by way of contrast, that no one cares about your birth or nurture or education, or, I may say, about that of any other Athenian, unless he has a lover who looks after him. And if you cast an eye on the wealth, the luxury, the garments with their flowing trains, the anointings with myrrh, the multitudes of attendants, and all the other bravery of the Persians, you will be ashamed when you discern your own inferiority; or if you look at the temperance and orderliness and ease and grace and magnanimity and courage and endurance and love of toil and desire of glory and ambition of the Lacedaemonians - in all these respects you will see that you are but a child in comparison of them. Even in the matter of wealth, if you value yourself upon that, I must reveal to you how you stand; for if you form an estimate of the wealth of the Lacedaemonians, you will see that our possessions fall far short of theirs. For no one here can compete with them either in the extent and fertility of their own and the Messenian territory, or in the number of their slaves, and especially of the Helots, or of their horses, or of the animals which feed on the Messenian pastures. But I have said enough of this: and as to gold and silver, there is more of them in Lacedaemon than in all the rest of Hellas, for during many generations gold has been always flowing in to them from the whole Hellenic world, and often from the barbarian also, and never going out, as in the fable of Aesop the fox said to the lion, 'The prints of the feet of those going in are distinct enough;' but who ever saw the trace of money going out of Lacedaemon? And therefore you may safely infer that the inhabitants are the richest of the Hellenes in gold and silver, and that their kings are the richest of them, for they have a larger share of these things, and they have also a tribute paid to them which is very considerable. Yet the Spartan wealth, though great in comparison of the wealth of the other Hellenes, is as nothing in comparison of that of the Persians and their kings. Why, I have been informed by a credible person who went up to the king (at Susa), that he passed through a large tract of excellent land, extending for nearly a day's journey, which the people of the country called the queen's girdle, and another, which they called her veil; and several other fair and fertile districts, which were reserved for the adornment of the queen, and are named after her several habiliments. Now, I cannot help thinking to myself, What if some one were to go to Amestris, the wife of Xerxes and mother of Artaxerxes, and say to her, There is a certain Dinomache, whose whole wardrobe is not worth fifty minae - and that will be more than the value - and she has a son who is possessed of a three-hundred acre patch at Erchiae, and he has a mind to go to war with your son - would she not wonder to what this Alcibiades trusts for success in the conflict? 'He must rely,' she would say to herself, 'upon his training and wisdom - these are the things which Hellenes value.' And if she heard that this Alcibiades who is making the attempt is not as yet twenty years old, and is wholly uneducated, and when his lover tells him that he ought to get education and training first, and then go and fight the king, he refuses, and says that he is well enough as he is, would she not be amazed, and ask 'On what, then, does the youth rely?' And if we replied: He relies on his beauty, and stature, and birth, and mental endowments, she would think that we were mad, Alcibiades, when she compared the advantages which you possess with those of her own people. And I believe that even Lampido, the daughter of Leotychides, the wife of Archidamus and mother of Agis, all of whom were kings, would have the same feeling; if, in your present uneducated state, you were to turn your thoughts against her son, she too would be equally astonished. But how disgraceful, that we should not have as high a notion of what is required in us as our enemies' wives and mothers have of the qualities which are required in their assai-lants! O my friend, be persuaded by me, and hear the Delphian inscription, 'Know thyself' - not the men whom you think, but these kings are our rivals, and we can only overcome them by pains and skill. And if you fail in the required qualities, you will fail also in beco-ming renowned among Hellenes and

Barbarians, which you seem to desire more than any other man ever desired anything.

ALCIBIADES: I entirely believe you; but what are the sort of pains which are required, Socrates, - can you tell me?

SOCRATES: Yes, I can; but we must take counsel together concerning the manner in which both of us may be most improved. For what I am telling you of the necessity of education applies to myself as well as to you; and there is only one point in which I have an advantage over you.

ALCIBIADES: What is that?

SOCRATES: I have a guardian who is better and wiser than your guardian, Pericles.

ALCIBIADES: Who is he, Socrates?

SOCRATES: God, Alcibiades, who up to this day has not allowed me to converse with you; and he inspires in me the faith that I am especially designed to bring you to honour.

ALCIBIADES: You are jesting, Socrates.

SOCRATES: Perhaps, at any rate, I am right

in saying that all men greatly need pains and care, and you and I above all men.

ALCIBIADES: You are not far wrong about me.

SOCRATES: And certainly not about myself.

ALCIBIADES: But what can we do?

SOCRATES: There must be no hesitation or cowardice, my friend.

ALCIBIADES: That would not become us, Socrates.

SOCRATES: No, indeed, and we ought to take counsel together: for do we not wish to be as good as possible?

ALCIBIADES: We do.

SOCRATES: In what sort of virtue?

ALCIBIADES: Plainly, in the virtue of good men.

SOCRATES: Who are good in what?

ALCIBIADES: Those, clearly, who are good in the management of affairs.

SOCRATES: What sort of affairs? Equestrian affairs?

ALCIBIADES: Certainly not.

SOCRATES: You mean that about them we should have recourse to horsemen?

ALCIBIADES: Yes.

SOCRATES: Well, naval affairs?

ALCIBIADES: No.

SOCRATES: You mean that we should have recourse to sailors about them?

ALCIBIADES: Yes.

SOCRATES: Then what affairs? And who do them?

ALCIBIADES: The affairs which occupy Athenian gentlemen.

SOCRATES: And when you speak of gentlemen, do you mean the wise or the unwise?

ALCIBIADES: The wise.

SOCRATES: And a man is good in respect of that in which he is wise?

ALCIBIADES: Yes.

SOCRATES: And evil in respect of that in which he is unwise?

ALCIBIADES: Certainly.

SOCRATES: The shoemaker, for example, is wise in respect of the making of shoes?

ALCIBIADES: Yes.

SOCRATES: Then he is good in that?

ALCIBIADES: He is.

SOCRATES: But in respect of the making of garments he is unwise?

ALCIBIADES: Yes.

SOCRATES: Then in that he is bad?

ALCIBIADES: Yes.

SOCRATES: Then upon this view of the matter the same man is good and also bad?

ALCIBIADES: True.

SOCRATES: But would you say that the good are the same as the bad?

ALCIBIADES: Certainly not.

SOCRATES: Then whom do you call the good?

ALCIBIADES: I mean by the good those who are able to rule in the city.

SOCRATES: Not, surely, over horses?

ALCIBIADES: Certainly not.

SOCRATES: But over men?

ALCIBIADES: Yes.

SOCRATES: When they are sick?

ALCIBIADES: No.

SOCRATES: Or on a voyage?

ALCIBIADES: No.

SOCRATES: Or reaping the harvest?

ALCIBIADES: No.

SOCRATES: When they are doing something or nothing?

ALCIBIADES: When they are doing something, I should say.

SOCRATES: I wish that you would explain to me what this something is.

ALCIBIADES: When they are having dealings with one another, and using one another's services, as we citizens do in our daily life.

SOCRATES: Those of whom you speak are ruling over men who are using the services of other men?

ALCIBIADES: Yes.

SOCRATES: Are they ruling over the signalmen who give the time to the rowers?

ALCIBIADES: No; they are not.

SOCRATES: That would be the office of the pilot?

ALCIBIADES: Yes.

SOCRATES: But, perhaps you mean that they rule over flute-players, who lead the singers and use the services of the dancers?

ALCIBIADES: Certainly not.

SOCRATES: That would be the business of the teacher of the chorus?

ALCIBIADES: Yes.

SOCRATES: Then what is the meaning of being able to rule over men who use other men?

ALCIBIADES: I mean that they rule over men who have common rights of citizenship, and dealings with one another.

SOCRATES: And what sort of an art is this? Suppose that I ask you again, as I did just now, What art makes men know how to rule over their fellow-sailors, - how would you answer?

ALCIBIADES: The art of the pilot.

SOCRATES: And, if I may recur to another old instance, what art enables them to rule over their fellow-singers?

ALCIBIADES: The art of the teacher of the chorus, which you were just now mentioning.

SOCRATES: And what do you call the art of fellow-citizens?

ALCIBIADES: I should say, good counsel, Socrates.

SOCRATES: And is the art of the pilot evil counsel?

ALCIBIADES: No.

SOCRATES: But good counsel?

ALCIBIADES: Yes, that is what I should say, - good counsel, of which the aim is the preservation of the voyagers.

SOCRATES: True. And what is the aim of that other good counsel of which you speak?

ALCIBIADES: The aim is the better order and preservation of the city.

SOCRATES: And what is that of which the absence or presence improves and preserves the order of the city? Suppose you were to ask me, what is that of which the presence or absence improves or preserves the order of the body? I should reply, the presence of health and the absence of disease. You would say the same?

ALCIBIADES: Yes.

SOCRATES: And if you were to ask me the same question about the eyes, I should reply in the same way, 'the presence of sight and the absence of blindness;' or about the ears, I should reply, that they were improved and were in better case, when deafness was absent, and hearing was present in them.

ALCIBIADES: True.

SOCRATES: And what would you say of a state? What is that by the presence or absence of which the state is improved and better managed and ordered?

ALCIBIADES: I should say, Socrates: - the presence of friendship and the absence of hatred and division.

SOCRATES: And do you mean by friendship agreement or disagreement?

ALCIBIADES: Agreement.

SOCRATES: What art makes cities agree about numbers?

ALCIBIADES: Arithmetic.

SOCRATES: And private individuals?

ALCIBIADES: The same.

SOCRATES: And what art makes each individual agree with himself?

ALCIBIADES: The same.

SOCRATES: And what art makes each of us agree with himself about the comparative length of the span and of the cubit? Does not the art of measure?

ALCIBIADES: Yes.

SOCRATES: Individuals are agreed with one another about this; and states, equally?

ALCIBIADES: Yes.

SOCRATES: And the same holds of the balance?

ALCIBIADES: True.

SOCRATES: But what is the other agreement of which you speak, and about what? what art can give that agreement? And does that which gives it to the state give it also to the individual, so as to make him consistent with himself and with another?

ALCIBIADES: I should suppose so.

SOCRATES: But what is the nature of the agreement? - answer, and faint not.

ALCIBIADES: I mean to say that there should be such friendship and agreement as exists between an affectionate father and mother and their son, or between brothers, or between husband and wife.

SOCRATES: But can a man, Alcibiades, agree with a woman about the spinning of wool, which she understands and he does not?

ALCIBIADES: No, truly.

SOCRATES: Nor has he any need, for spinning is a female accomplishment.

ALCIBIADES: Yes.

SOCRATES: And would a woman agree with

a man about the science of arms, which she has never learned?

ALCIBIADES: Certainly not.

SOCRATES: I suppose that the use of arms would be regarded by you as a male accomplishment?

ALCIBIADES: It would.

SOCRATES: Then, upon your view, women and men have two sorts of knowledge?

ALCIBIADES: Certainly.

SOCRATES: Then in their knowledge there is no agreement of women and men?

ALCIBIADES: There is not.

SOCRATES: Nor can there be friendship, if friendship is agreement?

ALCIBIADES: Plainly not.

SOCRATES: Then women are not loved by men when they do their own work?

ALCIBIADES: I suppose not.

SOCRATES: Nor men by women when they do their own work?

ALCIBIADES: No.

SOCRATES: Nor are states well administered, when individuals do their own work?

ALCIBIADES: I should rather think, Socrates, that the reverse is the truth. (Compare Republic.)

SOCRATES: What! do you mean to say that states are well administered when friendship is absent, the presence of which, as we were saying, alone secures their good order?

ALCIBIADES: But I should say that there is friendship among them, for this very reason, that the two parties respectively do their own work.

SOCRATES: That was not what you were saying before; and what do you mean now by affirming that friendship exists when there is no agreement? How can there be agreement about matters which the one party knows, and of which the other is in ignorance?

ALCIBIADES: Impossible.

SOCRATES: And when individuals are doing their own work, are they doing what is just or unjust?

ALCIBIADES: What is just, certainly.

SOCRATES: And when individuals do what is just in the state, is there no friendship among them?

ALCIBIADES: I suppose that there must be, Socrates.

SOCRATES: Then what do you mean by this friendship or agreement about which we must be wise and discreet in order that we may be good men? I cannot make out where it exists or among whom; according to you, the same persons may sometimes have it, and sometimes not.

ALCIBIADES: But, indeed, Socrates, I do not know what I am saying; and I have long been, unconsciously to myself, in a most disgraceful state.

SOCRATES: Nevertheless, cheer up; at fifty, if you had discovered your deficiency, you would have been too old, and the time for taking care of yourself would have passed away, but yours is just the age at which the discovery should be made.

ALCIBIADES: And what should he do, Socrates, who would make the discovery?

SOCRATES: Answer questions, Alcibiades; and that is a process which, by the grace of God, if I may put any faith in my oracle, will be very improving to both of us.

ALCIBIADES: If I can be improved by answering, I will answer.

SOCRATES: And first of all, that we may not peradventure be deceived by appearances, fancying, perhaps, that we are taking care of ourselves when we are not, what is the meaning of a man taking care of himself? and when does he take care? Does he take care of himself when he takes care of what belongs to him?

ALCIBIADES: I should think so.

SOCRATES: When does a man take care of his feet? Does he not take care of them when he takes care of that which belongs to his feet?

ALCIBIADES: I do not understand.

SOCRATES: Let me take the hand as an illustration; does not a ring belong to the finger, and to the finger only?

ALCIBIADES: Yes.

SOCRATES: And the shoe in like manner to the foot?

ALCIBIADES: Yes.

SOCRATES: And when we take care of our shoes, do we not take care of our feet?

ALCIBIADES: I do not comprehend, Socrates.

SOCRATES: But you would admit, Alcibiades, that to take proper care of a thing is a correct expression?

ALCIBIADES: Yes.

SOCRATES: And taking proper care means improving?

ALCIBIADES: Yes.

SOCRATES: And what is the art which improves our shoes?

ALCIBIADES: Shoemaking.

SOCRATES: Then by shoemaking we take care of our shoes?

ALCIBIADES: Yes.

SOCRATES: And do we by shoemaking take care of our feet, or by some other art which improves the feet?

ALCIBIADES: By some other art.

SOCRATES: And the same art improves the feet which improves the rest of the body?

ALCIBIADES: Very true.

SOCRATES: Which is gymnastic?

ALCIBIADES: Certainly.

SOCRATES: Then by gymnastic we take care of our feet, and by shoemaking of that which belongs to our feet?

ALCIBIADES: Very true.

SOCRATES: And by gymnastic we take care of our hands, and by the art of graving rings of that which belongs to our hands?

ALCIBIADES: Yes.

SOCRATES: And by gymnastic we take care of the body, and by the art of weaving and the other arts we take care of the things of the body?

ALCIBIADES: Clearly.

SOCRATES: Then the art which takes care of each thing is different from that which takes care of the belongings of each thing?

ALCIBIADES: True.

SOCRATES: Then in taking care of what belongs to you, you do not take care of yourself?

ALCIBIADES: Certainly not.

SOCRATES: For the art which takes care of our belongings appears not to be the same as that which takes care of ourselves?

ALCIBIADES: Clearly not.

SOCRATES: And now let me ask you what is the art with which we take care of ourselves?

ALCIBIADES: I cannot say.

SOCRATES: At any rate, thus much has been admitted, that the art is not one which makes any of our possessions, but which makes ourselves better?

ALCIBIADES: True.

SOCRATES: But should we ever have known what art makes a shoe better, if we did not know a shoe?

ALCIBIADES: Impossible.

SOCRATES: Nor should we know what art makes a ring better, if we did not know a ring?

ALCIBIADES: That is true.

SOCRATES: And can we ever know what art makes a man better, if we do not know what we are ourselves?

ALCIBIADES: Impossible.

SOCRATES: And is self-knowledge such an

easy thing, and was he to be lightly esteemed who inscribed the text on the temple at Delphi? Or is self-knowledge a difficult thing, which few are able to attain?

ALCIBIADES: At times I fancy, Socrates, that anybody can know himself; at other times the task appears to be very difficult.

SOCRATES: But whether easy or difficult, Alcibiades, still there is no other way; knowing what we are, we shall know how to take care of ourselves, and if we are ignorant we shall not know.

ALCIBIADES: That is true.

SOCRATES: Well, then, let us see in what way the self-existent can be discovered by us; that will give us a chance of discovering our own existence, which otherwise we can never know.

ALCIBIADES: You say truly.

SOCRATES: Come, now, I beseech you, tell me with whom you are conversing? - with whom but with me?

ALCIBIADES: Yes.

SOCRATES: As I am, with you?

ALCIBIADES: Yes.

SOCRATES: That is to say, I, Socrates, am talking?

ALCIBIADES: Yes.

SOCRATES: And Alcibiades is my hearer?

ALCIBIADES: Yes.

SOCRATES: And I in talking use words?

ALCIBIADES: Certainly.

SOCRATES: And talking and using words have, I suppose, the same meaning?

ALCIBIADES: To be sure.

SOCRATES: And the user is not the same as the thing which he uses?

ALCIBIADES: What do you mean?

SOCRATES: I will explain; the shoemaker, for example, uses a square tool, and a circular tool, and other tools for cutting?

ALCIBIADES: Yes.

SOCRATES: But the tool is not the same as the cutter and user of the tool?

ALCIBIADES: Of course not.

SOCRATES: And in the same way the instrument of the harper is to be distinguished from the harper himself?

ALCIBIADES: It is.

SOCRATES: Now the question which I asked was whether you conceive the user to be always different from that which he uses?

ALCIBIADES: I do.

SOCRATES: Then what shall we say of the shoemaker? Does he cut with his tools only or with his hands?

ALCIBIADES: With his hands as well.

SOCRATES: He uses his hands too?

ALCIBIADES: Yes.

SOCRATES: And does he use his eyes in cutting leather?

ALCIBIADES: He does.

SOCRATES: And we admit that the user is not the same with the things which he uses?

ALCIBIADES: Yes.

SOCRATES: Then the shoemaker and the harper are to be distinguished from the hands and feet which they use?

ALCIBIADES: Clearly.

SOCRATES: And does not a man use the whole body?

ALCIBIADES: Certainly.

SOCRATES: And that which uses is different from that which is used?

ALCIBIADES: True.

SOCRATES: Then a man is not the same as his own body?

ALCIBIADES: That is the inference.

SOCRATES: What is he, then?

ALCIBIADES: I cannot say.

SOCRATES: Nay, you can say that he is the user of the body.

ALCIBIADES: Yes.

SOCRATES: And the user of the body is the soul?

ALCIBIADES: Yes, the soul.

SOCRATES: And the soul rules?

ALCIBIADES: Yes.

SOCRATES: Let me make an assertion which will, I think, be universally admitted.

ALCIBIADES: What is it?

SOCRATES: That man is one of three things.

ALCIBIADES: What are they?

SOCRATES: Soul, body, or both together forming a whole.

ALCIBIADES: Certainly.

SOCRATES: But did we not say that the actual ruling principle of the body is man?

ALCIBIADES: Yes, we did.

SOCRATES: And does the body rule over itself?

ALCIBIADES: Certainly not.

SOCRATES: It is subject, as we were saying?

ALCIBIADES: Yes.

SOCRATES: Then that is not the principle which we are seeking?

ALCIBIADES: It would seem not.

SOCRATES: But may we say that the union of the two rules over the body, and conesquently that this is man?

ALCIBIADES: Very likely.

SOCRATES: The most unlikely of all things; for if one of the members is subject, the two united cannot possibly rule.

ALCIBIADES: True.

SOCRATES: But since neither the body, nor the union of the two, is man, either man has no real existence, or the soul is man?

ALCIBIADES: Just so.

SOCRATES: Is anything more required to prove that the soul is man?

ALCIBIADES: Certainly not; the proof is, I think, quite sufficient.

SOCRATES: And if the proof, although not perfect, be sufficient, we shall be satisfied; - more precise proof will be supplied when we have discovered that which we were led to omit, from a fear that the enquiry would be too much protracted.

ALCIBIADES: What was that?

SOCRATES: What I meant, when I said that absolute existence must be first considered; but now, instead of absolute existence, we have been considering the nature of individual existence, and this may, perhaps, be sufficient; for surely there is nothing which may be called more properly ourselves than the soul?

ALCIBIADES: There is nothing.

SOCRATES: Then we may truly conceive that you and I are conversing with one another, soul to soul?

ALCIBIADES: Very true.

SOCRATES: And that is just what I was saying before - that I, Socrates, am not arguing or talking with the face of Alcibiades, but with the real Alcibiades; or in other words, with his soul.

ALCIBIADES: True.

SOCRATES: Then he who bids a man know himself, would have him know his soul?

ALCIBIADES: That appears to be true.

SOCRATES: He whose knowledge only extends to the body, knows the things of a man, and not the man himself?

ALCIBIADES: That is true.

SOCRATES: Then neither the physician regarded as a physician, nor the trainer regarded as a trainer, knows himself?

ALCIBIADES: He does not.

SOCRATES: The husbandmen and the other craftsmen are very far from knowing themselves, for they would seem not even to know their own belongings? When regarded in relation to the arts which they practise they are even further removed from self-knowledge, for they only know the belongings of the body, which minister to the body.

ALCIBIADES: That is true.

SOCRATES: Then if temperance is the knowledge of self, in respect of his art none of them is temperate?

ALCIBIADES: I agree.

SOCRATES: And this is the reason why their arts are accounted vulgar, and are not such as a good man would practise?

ALCIBIADES: Quite true.

SOCRATES: Again, he who cherishes his body cherishes not himself, but what belongs to him?

ALCIBIADES: That is true.

SOCRATES: But he who cherishes his money, cherishes neither himself nor his belongings, but is in a stage yet further removed from himself?

ALCIBIADES: I agree.

SOCRATES: Then the money-maker has really ceased to be occupied with his own concerns?

ALCIBIADES: True.

SOCRATES: And if any one has fallen in love with the person of Alcibiades, he loves not Alcibiades, but the belongings of Alcibiades?

ALCIBIADES: True.

SOCRATES: But he who loves your soul is the true lover?

ALCIBIADES: That is the necessary inference.

SOCRATES: The lover of the body goes away when the flower of youth fades?

ALCIBIADES: True.

SOCRATES: But he who loves the soul goes not away, as long as the soul follows after virtue?

ALCIBIADES: Yes.

SOCRATES: And I am the lover who goes

not away, but remains with you, when you are no longer young and the rest are gone?

ALCIBIADES: Yes, Socrates; and therein you do well, and I hope that you will remain.

SOCRATES: Then you must try to look your best.

ALCIBIADES: I will.

SOCRATES: The fact is, that there is only one lover of Alcibiades the son of Cleinias; there neither is nor ever has been seemingly any other; and he is his darling, - Socrates, the son of Sophroniscus and Phaenarete.

ALCIBIADES: True.

SOCRATES: And did you not say, that if I had not spoken first, you were on the point of coming to me, and enquiring why I only remained?

ALCIBIADES: That is true.

SOCRATES: The reason was that I loved you for your own sake, whereas other men love what belongs to you; and your beauty, which is not you, is fading away, just as your true self is beginning to bloom. And I will never desert you, if you are not spoiled and deformed by the Athenian people; for the danger which I most fear is that you will become a lover of the people and will be spoiled by them. Many a noble Athenian has been ruined in this way. For the demus of the great-hearted Erechteus is of a fair countenance, but you should see him naked; wherefore observe the caution which I give you.

ALCIBIADES: What caution?

SOCRATES: Practise yourself, sweet friend, in learning what you ought to know, before you enter on politics; and then you will have an antidote which will keep you out of harm's way.

ALCIBIADES: Good advice, Socrates, but I wish that you would explain to me in what way I am to take care of myself.

SOCRATES: Have we not made an advance? for we are at any rate tolerably well agreed as to what we are, and there is no longer any danger, as we once feared, that we might be taking care not of ourselves, but of something which is not ourselves.

ALCIBIADES: That is true.

SOCRATES: And the next step will be to take care of the soul, and look to that?

ALCIBIADES: Certainly.

SOCRATES: Leaving the care of our bodies and of our properties to others?

ALCIBIADES: Very good.

SOCRATES: But how can we have a perfect knowledge of the things of the soul? - For if we know them, then I suppose we shall know ourselves. Can we really be ignorant of the excellent meaning of the Delphian inscription, of which we were just now speaking?

ALCIBIADES: What have you in your thoughts, Socrates?

SOCRATES: I will tell you what I suspect to be the meaning and lesson of that inscription. Let me take an illustration from sight, which I imagine to be the only one suitable to my purpose.

ALCIBIADES: What do you mean?

SOCRATES: Consider; if some one were to say to the eye, 'See thyself,' as you might say to a man, 'Know thyself,' what is the nature and meaning ofthis precept? Would not his meaning be: - That the eye should look at that in which it would see itself?

ALCIBIADES: Clearly.

SOCRATES: And what are the objects in looking at which we see ourselves?

ALCIBIADES: Clearly, Socrates, in looking at mirrors and the like.

SOCRATES: Very true; and is there not something of the nature of a mirror in our own eyes?

ALCIBIADES: Certainly.

SOCRATES: Did you ever observe that the face of the person looking into the eye of another is reflected as in a mirror; and in the visual organ which is over against him, and which is called the pupil, there is a sort of image of the person looking?

ALCIBIADES: That is quite true.

SOCRATES: Then the eye, looking at another eye, and at that in the eye which is most perfect, and which is the instrument of vision, will there see itself?

ALCIBIADES: That is evident.

SOCRATES: But looking at anything else either in man or in the world, and not to what resembles this, it will not see itself?

ALCIBIADES: Very true.

SOCRATES: Then if the eye is to see itself, it must look at the eye, and at that part of the eye where sight which is the virtue of the eye resides?

ALCIBIADES: True.

SOCRATES: And if the soul, my dear Alcibiades, is ever to know herself, must she not look at the soul; and especially at that part of the soul in which her virtue resides, and to any other which is like this?

ALCIBIADES: I agree, Socrates.

SOCRATES: And do we know of any part of our souls more divine than that which has to do with wisdom and knowledge?

ALCIBIADES: There is none.

SOCRATES: Then this is that part of the soul

which resembles the divine; and he who looks at this and at the whole class of things divine, will be most likely to know himself?

ALCIBIADES: Clearly.

SOCRATES: And self-knowledge we agree to be wisdom?

ALCIBIADES: True.

SOCRATES: But if we have no self-knowledge and no wisdom, can we ever know our own good and evil?

ALCIBIADES: How can we, Socrates?

SOCRATES: You mean, that if you did not know Alcibiades, there would be no possibility of your knowing that what belonged to to Alcibiades was really his?

ALCIBIADES: It would be quite impossible.

SOCRATES: Nor should we know that we were the persons to whom anything belonged, if we did not know ourselves?

ALCIBIADES: How could we?

SOCRATES: And if we did not know our own belongings, neither should we know the belongings of our belongings?

ALCIBIADES: Clearly not.

SOCRATES: Then we were not altogether right in acknowledging just now that a man may know what belongs to him and yet not know himself; nay, rather he cannot even know the belongings of his belongings; for the discernment of the things of self, and of the things which belong to the things of self, appear all to be the business of the same man, and of the same art.

ALCIBIADES: So much may be supposed.

SOCRATES: And he who knows not the things which belong to himself, will in like manner be ignorant of the things which belong to others?

ALCIBIADES: Very true.

SOCRATES: And if he knows not the affairs of others, he will not know the affairs of states?

ALCIBIADES: Certainly not.

SOCRATES: Then such a man can never be a statesman?

ALCIBIADES: He cannot.

SOCRATES: Nor an economist?

ALCIBIADES: He cannot.

SOCRATES: He will not know what he is doing?

ALCIBIADES: He will not.

SOCRATES: And will not he who is ignorant fall into error?

ALCIBIADES: Assuredly.

SOCRATES: And if he falls into error will he not fail both in his public and private capacity?

ALCIBIADES: Yes, indeed.

SOCRATES: And failing, will he not be miserable?

ALCIBIADES: Very.

SOCRATES: And what will become of those

for whom he is acting?

ALCIBIADES: They will be miserable also.

SOCRATES: Then he who is not wise and good cannot be happy?

ALCIBIADES: He cannot.

SOCRATES: The bad, then, are miserable?

ALCIBIADES: Yes, very.

SOCRATES: And if so, not he who has riches, but he who has wisdom, is delivered from his misery?

ALCIBIADES: Clearly.

SOCRATES: Cities, then, if they are to be happy, do not want walls, or triremes, or docks, or numbers, or size, Alcibiades, without virtue? (Compare Arist. Pol.)

ALCIBIADES: Indeed they do not.

SOCRATES: And you must give the citizens virtue, if you mean to administer their affairs rightly or nobly?

ALCIBIADES: Certainly.

SOCRATES: But can a man give that which he has not?

ALCIBIADES: Impossible.

SOCRATES: Then you or any one who means to govern and superintend, not only himself and the things of himself, but the state and the things of the state, must in the first place acquire virtue.

ALCIBIADES: That is true.

SOCRATES: You have not therefore to obtain power or authority, in order to enable you to do what you wish for yourself and the state, but justice and wisdom.

ALCIBIADES: Clearly.

SOCRATES: You and the state, if you act wisely and justly, will act according to the will of God?

ALCIBIADES: Certainly.

SOCRATES: As I was saying before, you will look only at what is bright and divine, and act with a view to them?

ALCIBIADES: Yes.

SOCRATES: In that mirror you will see and know yourselves and your own good?

ALCIBIADES: Yes.

SOCRATES: And so you will act rightly and well?

ALCIBIADES: Yes.

SOCRATES: In which case, I will be security for your happiness.

ALCIBIADES: I accept the security.

SOCRATES: But if you act unrighteously, your eye will turn to the dark and godless, and being in darkness and ignorance of your-elves, you will probably do deeds of darkness.

ALCIBIADES: Very possibly.

SOCRATES: For if a man, my dear Alci-biades, has the power to do what he likes, but has no understanding, what is likely to be the result, either to him as an individual or to the state - for example, if he be sick and is able to do what he likes, not having the mind of a physician -having moreover tyrannical power, and no one daring to reprove him, what will happen to him? Will he not be likely to have his constitution ruined?

ALCIBIADES: That is true.

SOCRATES: Or again, in a ship, if a man having the power to do what he likes, has no intelligence or skill in navigation, do you see what will happen to him and to his fellow-sailors?

ALCIBIADES: Yes; I see that they will all perish.

SOCRATES: And in like manner, in a state, and where there is any power and authority which is wanting in virtue, will not misfortune, in like manner, ensue?

ALCIBIADES: Certainly.

SOCRATES: Not tyrannical power, then, my good Alcibiades, should be the aim either of individuals or states, if they would be happy, but virtue.

ALCIBIADES: That is true.

SOCRATES: And before they have virtue, to be commanded by a superior is better for men as well as for children? (Compare Arist. Pol.)

ALCIBIADES: That is evident.

SOCRATES: And that which is better is also nobler?

ALCIBIADES: True.

SOCRATES: And what is nobler is more becoming?

ALCIBIADES: Certainly.

SOCRATES: Then to the bad man slavery is more becoming, because better?

ALCIBIADES: True.

SOCRATES: Then vice is only suited to a slave?

ALCIBIADES: Yes.

SOCRATES: And virtue to a freeman?

ALCIBIADES: Yes.

SOCRATES: And, O my friend, is not the condition of a slave to be avoided?

ALCIBIADES: Certainly, Socrates.

SOCRATES: And are you now conscious of your own state? And do you know whether you are a freeman or not?

ALCIBIADES: I think that I am very conscious indeed of my own state.

SOCRATES: And do you know how to escape out of a state which I do not even like to name to my beauty?

ALCIBIADES: Yes, I do.

SOCRATES: How?

ALCIBIADES: By your help, Socrates.

SOCRATES: That is not well said, Alcibiades.

ALCIBIADES: What ought I to have said?

SOCRATES: By the help of God.

ALCIBIADES: I agree; and I further say, that our relations are likely to be reversed. From this day forward, I must and will follow you as you have followed me; I will be the disciple, and you shall be my master.

SOCRATES: O that is rare! My love breeds

another love: and so like the stork I shall be cherished by the bird whom I have hatched.

ALCIBIADES: Strange, but true; and henceforward I shall begin to think about justice.

SOCRATES: And I hope that you will persist; although I have fears, not because I doubt you; but I see the power of the state, which may be too much for both of us.

ALCIBIADES II

(see Appendix II)

PERSONS OF THE DIALOGUE: Socrates, Alcibiades

SOCRATES: Are you going, Alcibiades, to offer prayer to Zeus?

ALCIBIADES: Yes, Socrates, I am.

SOCRATES: you seem to be troubled and to cast your eyes on the ground, as though you were thinking about something.

ALCIBIADES: Of what do you suppose that I am thinking?

SOCRATES: Of the greatest of all things, as I believe. Tell me, do you not suppose that the Gods sometimes partly grant and partly reject the requests which we make in public and private, and favour some persons and not others?

ALCIBIADES: Certainly.

SOCRATES: Do you not imagine, then, that a man ought to be very careful, lest perchance without knowing it he implore great evils for himself, deeming that he is asking for good, especially if the Gods are in the mood to grant whatever he may request? There is the story of Oedipus, for instance, who prayed that his children might divide their inheritance between them by the sword: he did not, as he might have done, beg that his present evils might be averted, but called down new ones. And was not his prayer accomplished, and did not many and terrible evils thence arise, upon which I need not dilate?

ALCIBIADES: Yes, Socrates, but you are speaking of a madman: surely you do not think that any one in his senses would venture to make such a prayer?

SOCRATES: Madness, then, you consider to be the opposite of discretion?

ALCIBIADES: Of course.

SOCRATES: And some men seem to you to be discreet, and others the contrary?

ALCIBIADES: They do.

SOCRATES: Well, then, let us discuss who

these are. We acknowledge that some are discreet, some foolish, and that some are mad?

ALCIBIADES: Yes.

SOCRATES: And again, there are some who are in health?

ALCIBIADES: There are.

SOCRATES: While others are ailing?

ALCIBIADES: Yes.

SOCRATES: And they are not the same?

ALCIBIADES: Certainly not.

SOCRATES: Nor are there any who are in neither state?

ALCIBIADES: No.

SOCRATES: A man must either be sick or be well?

ALCIBIADES: That is my opinion.

SOCRATES: Very good: and do you think the same about discretion and want of discretion?

ALCIBIADES: How do you mean?

SOCRATES: Do you believe that a man must be either in or out of his senses; or is there some third or intermediate condition, in which he is neither one nor the other?

ALCIBIADES: Decidedly not.

SOCRATES: He must be either sane or insane?

ALCIBIADES: So I suppose.

SOCRATES: Did you not acknowledge that madness was the opposite of discretion?

ALCIBIADES: Yes.

SOCRATES: And that there is no third or middle term between discretion and indiscretion?

ALCIBIADES: True.

SOCRATES: And there cannot be two opposites to one thing?

ALCIBIADES: There cannot.

SOCRATES: Then madness and want of sense are the same?

ALCIBIADES: That appears to be the case.

SOCRATES: We shall be in the right, therefore, Alcibiades, if we say that all who are senseless are mad. For example, if among persons of your own age or older than yourself there are some who are senseless, - as there certainly are, - they are mad. For tell me, by heaven, do you not think that in the city the wise are few, while the foolish, whom you call mad, are many?

ALCIBIADES: I do.

SOCRATES: But how could we live in safety with so many crazy people? Should we not long since have paid the penalty at their hands, and have been struck and beaten and endured every other form of ill-usage which madmen are wont to inflict? Consider, my dear friend: may it not be quite otherwise?

ALCIBIADES: Why, Socrates, how is that possible? I must have been mistaken.

SOCRATES: So it seems to me. But perhaps we may consider the matter thus: -

ALCIBIADES: How?

SOCRATES: I will tell you. We think that some are sick; do we not?

ALCIBIADES: Yes.

SOCRATES: And must every sick person either have the gout, or be in a fever, or suffer from ophthalmia? Or do you believe that a man may labour under some other disease, even although he has none of these complaints? Surely, they are not the only maladies which exist?

ALCIBIADES: Certainly not.

SOCRATES: And is every kind of opthalmia a disease?

ALCIBIADES: Yes.

SOCRATES: And every disease ophthalmia?

ALCIBIADES: Surely not. But I scarcely understand what I mean myself.

SOCRATES: Perhaps, if you give me your best attention, 'two of us' looking together, we may find what we seek.

ALCIBIADES: I am attending, Socrates, to the best of my power.

SOCRATES: We are agreed, then, that every form of ophthalmia is a disease, but not every disease ophthalmia?

ALCIBIADES: We are.

SOCRATES: And so far we seem to be right. For every one who suffers from a fever is sick; but the sick, I conceive, do not all have fever or gout or ophthalmia, although each of these is a disease, which, according to those whom we call physicians, may require a different treatment. They are not all alike, nor do they produce the same result, but each has its own effect, and yet they are all diseases. May we not take an illustration from the artizans?

ALCIBIADES: Certainly.

SOCRATES: There are cobblers and carpenters and sculptors and others of all sorts and kinds, whom we need not stop to enumerate. All have their distinct employments and all are workmen, although they are not all of them cobblers or carpenters or sculptors.

ALCIBIADES: No, indeed.

SOCRATES: And in like manner men differ in regard to want of sense. Those who are most out of their wits we call 'madmen,' while we term those who are less far gone 'stupid' or 'idiotic,' or, if we prefer gentler language, describe them as 'romantic' or 'simple-minded,' or, again, as 'innocent' or 'inexperienced' or 'foolish.' You may even find other names, if you seek for them; but by all of them lack of sense is intended. They only differ as one art appeared to us to differ from another or one disease from another. Or what is your opinion?

ALCIBIADES: I agree with you.

SOCRATES: Then let us return to the point at which we digressed. We said at first that we should have to consider who were the wise and who the foolish. For we acknowledged that there are these two classes? Did we not?

ALCIBIADES: To be sure.

SOCRATES: And you regard those as sensible who know what ought to be done or said?

ALCIBIADES: Yes.

SOCRATES: The senseless are those who do not know this?

ALCIBIADES: True.

SOCRATES: The latter will say or do what they ought not without their own knowledge?

ALCIBIADES: Exactly.

SOCRATES: Oedipus, as I was saying, Alcibiades, was a person of this sort. And even now-a-days you will find many who (have offered inauspicious prayers), although, unlike him, they were not in anger nor thought that they were asking evil. He neither sought, nor supposed that he sought for good, but others have had quite the contrary notion. I believe that if the God whom you are about to consult should appear to you, and, in anticipation of your request, enquired whether you would be contented to become tyrant of Athens, and if this seemed in your eyes a small and mean thing, should add to it the dominion of all Hellas; and seeing that even then you would not be satisfied unless you were ruler of the whole of Europe, should promise, not only that, but, if you so desired, should proclaim to all mankind in one and the same day that Alcibiades, son of Cleinias, was tyrant: - in such a case, I imagine, you would depart full of joy, as one who had obtained the greatest of goods.

ALCIBIADES: And not only I, Socrates, but any one else who should meet with such luck.

SOCRATES: Yet you would not accept the dominion and lordship of all the Hellenes and all the barbarians in exchange for your life?

ALCIBIADES: Certainly not: for then what use could I make of them?

SOCRATES: And would you accept them if you were likely to use them to a bad and mischievous end?

ALCIBIADES: I would not.

SOCRATES: You see that it is not safe for a man either rashly to accept whatever is offered him, or himself to request a thing, if he is likely to suffer thereby or immediately to lose his life. And yet we could tell of many who, having long desired and diligently laboured to obtain a tyranny, thinking that thus they would procure an advantage, have nevertheless fallen victims to designing enemies. You must have heard of what happened only the other day, how Archelaus of Macedonia was slain by his beloved (compare Aristotle, Pol.), whose love for the tyranny was not less than that of Archelaus for him. The tyrannicide expected by his crime to become tyrant and afterwards to have a happy life; but when he had held the tyranny three or four days, he was in his turn conspired against and slain. Or look at certain of our own citizens, - and of their actions we have been not hearers, but eyewitnesses, - who have desired to obtain military command: of those who have gained their object, some are even to this day exiles from the city, while others have lost their lives. And even they who seem to have fared best, have not only gone through many perils and terrors during their office, but after their return home they have been beset by informers worse than they once were by their foes, insomuch that several of them have wished that they had remained in a private station rather than have had the glories of command. If, indeed, such perils and terrors were of profit to the commonwealth, there would be reason in undergoing them; but the very contrary is the case. Again, you will find persons who have prayed for offspring, and when their prayers were heard, have fallen into the greatest pains and sufferings. For some have begotten children who were utterly bad, and have therefore passed all their days in misery, while the parents of good children have undergone the misfortune of losing them, and have been so little happier than the others that they would have preferred never to have had children rather than to have had them and lost them. And yet, although these and the like examples are manifest and known of all, it is rare to find any one who has refused what has been offered him, or, if he were likely to gain aught by prayer, has refrained from making his petition. The mass of mankind would not decline to accept a tyranny, or the command of an army, or any of the numerous things which cause more harm than good: but rather, if they had them not, would have prayed to obtain them. And often in a short space of time they change their tone, and wish their old prayers unsaid. Wherefore also I suspect that men are entirely wrong when they blame the gods as the authors of the ills which befall them (compare Republic): 'their own presumption,' or folly (whichever is the right word) -

'Has brought these unmeasured woes upon them.' (Homer. Odyss.)

He must have been a wise poet, Alcibiades, who, seeing as I believe, his friends foolishly praying for and doing things which would not really profit them, offered up a common prayer in behalf of them all: -

'King Zeus, grant us good whether prayed for or unsought by us; But that which we ask amiss, do thou avert.' (The author of these lines, which are probably of Pythagorean origin, is unknown. They are found also in the Anthology (Anth. Pal.).)

In my opinion, I say, the poet spoke both well and prudently; but if you have anything to say in answer to him, speak out.

ALCIBIADES: It is difficult, Socrates, to oppose what has been well said. And I perceive how many are the ills of which ignorance is the cause, since, as would appear, through ignorance we not only do, but what is worse, pray for the greatest evils. No man would imagine that he would do so; he would rather suppose that he was quite capable of praying for what was best: to call down evils seems more like a curse than a prayer.

SOCRATES: But perhaps, my good friend, some one who is wiser than either you or I will say that we have no right to blame ignorance thus rashly, unless we can add what ignorance we mean and of what, and also to whom and how it is respectively a good or an evil?

ALCIBIADES: How do you mean? Can ignorance possibly be better than knowledge for any person in any conceivable case?

SOCRATES: So I believe: - you do not think so?

ALCIBIADES: Certainly not.

SOCRATES: And yet surely I may not suppose that you would ever wish to act towards your mother as they say that Orestes and Alcmeon and others have done towards their parent.

ALCIBIADES: Good words, Socrates, prithee.

SOCRATES: You ought not to bid him use auspicious words, who says that you would not be willing to commit so horrible a deed, but rather him who affirms the contrary, if the act appear to you unfit even to be mentioned. Or do you think that Orestes, had he been in his senses and knew what was best for him to do, would ever have dared to venture on such a crime?

ALCIBIADES: Certainly not.

SOCRATES: Nor would any one else, I fancy?

ALCIBIADES: No.

SOCRATES: That ignorance is bad then, it would appear, which is of the best and does not know what is best?

ALCIBIADES: So I think, at least.

SOCRATES: And both to the person who is ignorant and everybody else?

ALCIBIADES: Yes.

SOCRATES: Let us take another case. Suppose that you were suddenly to get into your head that it would be a good thing to kill Pericles, your kinsman and guardian, and were to seize a sword and, going to the doors of his house, were to enquire if he were at home, meaning to slay only him and no one else: - the servants reply, 'Yes': (Mind, I do not mean that you would really do such a thing; but there is nothing, you think, to prevent a man who is ignorant of the best, having occasionally the whim that what is worst is best?

ALCIBIADES: No.

SOCRATES: - If, then, you went indoors, and seeing him, did not know him, but thought that he was some one else, would you venture to slay him?

ALCIBIADES: Most decidedly not (it seems to me). (These words are omitted in several MSS.)

SOCRATES: For you designed to kill, not the first who offered, but Pericles himself?

ALCIBIADES: Certainly.

SOCRATES: And if you made many attempts, and each time failed to recognize Pericles, you would never attack him?

ALCIBIADES: Never.

SOCRATES: Well, but if Orestes in like manner had not known his mother, do you think that he would ever have laid hands upon her?

ALCIBIADES: No.

SOCRATES: He did not intend to slay the first woman he came across, nor any one else's mother, but only his own?

ALCIBIADES: True.

SOCRATES: Ignorance, then, is better for those who are in such a frame of mind, and have such ideas?

ALCIBIADES: Obviously.

SOCRATES: You acknowledge that for some persons in certain cases the ignorance of some things is a good and not an evil, as you formerly supposed?

ALCIBIADES: I do.

SOCRATES: And there is still another case which will also perhaps appear strange to you, if you will consider it? (The reading is here uncertain.)

ALCIBIADES: What is that, Socrates?

SOCRATES: It may be, in short, that the possession of all the sciences, if unaccompanied by the knowledge of the best, will more often than not injure the possessor. Consider the matter thus: - Must we not, when we intend either to do or say anything, suppose that we know or ought to know that which we propose so confidently to do or say?

ALCIBIADES: Yes, in my opinion.

SOCRATES: We may take the orators for an example, who from time to time advise us about war and peace, or the building of walls and the construction of harbours, whether they understand the business in hand, or only think that they do. Whatever the city, in a word, does to another city, or in the management of her own affairs, all happens by the counsel of the orators.

ALCIBIADES: True.

SOCRATES: But now see what follows, if I can (make it clear to you). (Some words appear to have dropped out here.) You would distinguish the wise from the foolish?

ALCIBIADES: Yes.

SOCRATES: The many are foolish, the few wise?

ALCIBIADES: Certainly.

SOCRATES: And you use both the terms, 'wise' and 'foolish,' in reference to something?

ALCIBIADES: I do.

SOCRATES: Would you call a person wise who can give advice, but does not know whether or when it is better to carry out the advice?

ALCIBIADES: Decidedly not.

SOCRATES: Nor again, I suppose, a person who knows the art of war, but does not know whether it is better to go to war or for how long?

ALCIBIADES: No.

SOCRATES: Nor, once more, a person who knows how to kill another or to take away his property or to drive him from his native land, but not when it is better to do so or for whom it is better?

ALCIBIADES: Certainly not.

SOCRATES: But he who understands anything of the kind and has at the same time the knowledge of the best course of action: - and the best and the useful are surely the same? -

ALCIBIADES: Yes.

SOCRATES: -Such an one, I say, we should call wise and a useful adviser both of himself and of the city. What do you think?

ALCIBIADES: I agree.

SOCRATES: And if any one knows how to ride or to shoot with the bow or to box or to wrestle, or to engage in any other sort of contest or to do anything whatever which is in the nature of an art, -what do you call him who knows what is best according to that art? Do you not speak of one who knows what is best in riding as a good rider?

ALCIBIADES: Yes.

SOCRATES: And in a similar way you speak of a good boxer or a good flute-player or a good performer in any other art?

ALCIBIADES: True.

SOCRATES: But is it necessary that the man who is clever in any of these arts should be wise also in general? Or is there a difference between the clever artist and the wise man?

ALCIBIADES: All the difference in the world.

SOCRATES: And what sort of a state do you think that would be which was composed of good archers and flute-players and athletes and masters in other arts, and besides them of those others about whom we spoke, who knew how to go to war and how to kill, as well as of orators puffed up with political pride, but in which not one of them all had this knowledge of the best, and there was no one who could tell when it was better to apply any of these arts or in regard to whom?

ALCIBIADES: I should call such a state bad, Socrates.

SOCRATES: You certainly would when you saw each of them rivalling the other and esteeming that of the greatest importance in the state, 'Wherein he himself most excelled.' (Euripides, Antiope.)

- I mean that which was best in any art, while he was entirely ignorant of what was best for himself and for the state, because, as I think, he trusts to opinion which is devoid of intelligence. In such a case should we not be right if we said that the state would be full of anarchy and lawlessness?

ALCIBIADES: Decidedly.

SOCRATES: But ought we not then, think you, either to fancy that we know or really to know, what we confidently propose to do or say?

ALCIBIADES: Yes.

SOCRATES: And if a person does that which he knows or supposes that he knows, and the result is beneficial, he will act advantageously both for himself and for the state?

ALCIBIADES: True.

SOCRATES: And if he do the contrary, both he and the state will suffer?

ALCIBIADES: Yes.

SOCRATES: Well, and are you of the same mind, as before?

ALCIBIADES: I am.

SOCRATES: But were you not saying that you would call the many unwise and the few wise?

ALCIBIADES: I was.

SOCRATES: And have we not come back to our old assertion that the many fail to obtain the best because they trust to opinion which is devoid of intelligence?

ALCIBIADES: That is the case.

SOCRATES: It is good, then, for the many, if

they particularly desire to do that which they know or suppose that they know, neither to know nor to suppose that they know, in cases where if they carry out their ideas in action they will be losers rather than gainers?

ALCIBIADES: What you say is very true.

SOCRATES: Do you not see that I was really speaking the truth when I affirmed that the possession of any other kind of knowledge was more likely to injure than to benefit the possessor, unless he had also the knowledge of the best?

ALCIBIADES: I do now, if I did not before, Socrates.

SOCRATES: The state or the soul, therefore, which wishes to have a right existence must hold firmly to this knowledge, just as the sick man clings to the physician, or the passenger depends for safety on the pilot. And if the soul does not set sail until she have obtained this she will be all the safer in the voyage through life. But when she rushes in pursuit of wealth or bodily strength or anything else, not having the knowledge of the best, so much the more is she likely to meet with misfortune. And he who has the love of learning (Or, reading polumatheian, 'abundant learning.'), and is skilful in many arts, and does not possess the knowledge of the best, but is under some other guidance, will make, as he deserves, a sorry voyage: - he will, I believe, hurry through the brief space of human life, pilotless in mid-ocean, and the words will apply to him in which the poet blamed his enemy: -

'...Full many a thing he knew; But knew them all badly.' (A fragment from the pseudo-Homeric poem, 'Margites.')

ALCIBIADES: How in the world, Socrates, do the words of the poet apply to him? They seem to me to have no bearing on the point whatever.

SOCRATES: Quite the contrary, my sweet friend: only the poet is talking in riddles after the fashion of his tribe. For all poetry has by nature an enigmatical character, and it is by no means everybody who can interpret it. And if, moreover, the spirit of poetry happen to seize on a man who is of a begrudging temper and does not care to manifest his wisdom but keeps it to himself as far as he can, it does indeed require an almost superhuman wisdom to discover what the poet would be at. You surely do not suppose that Homer, the wisest and most divine of poets, was unaware of the impossibility of knowing a thing badly: for it was no less a person than he who said of Margites that 'he knew many things, but knew them all badly.' The solution of the riddle is this, I imagine: - By 'badly' Homer meant 'bad' and 'knew' stands for 'to know.' Put the words together; - the metre will suffer, but the poet's meaning is clear; - 'Margites knew all these things, but it was bad for him to know them.' And, obviously, if it was bad for him to know so many things, he must have been a good-for-nothing, unless the argument has played us false.

ALCIBIADES: But I do not think that it has, Socrates: at least, if the argument is fallacious, it would be difficult for me to find another which I could trust.

SOCRATES: And you are right in thinking so.

ALCIBIADES: Well, that is my opinion.

SOCRATES: But tell me, by Heaven: - you must see now the nature and greatness of the difficulty in which you, like others, have your part. For you change about in all directions, and never come to rest anywhere: what you once most strongly inclined to suppose, you put aside again and quite alter your mind. If the God to whose shrine you are going should appear at this moment, and ask before you made your prayer, 'Whether you would desire to have one of the things which we mentioned at first, or whether he should leave you to make your own request:' - what in either case, think you, would be the best way to take advantage of the opportunity?

ALCIBIADES: Indeed, Socrates, I could not answer you without consideration. It seems to me to be a wild thing (The Homeric word margos is said to be here employed in allusion to the quotation from the 'Margites' which Socrates has just made; but it is not used in the sense which it has in Homer.) to make such a request; a man must be very careful lest he pray for evil under the idea that he is asking for good, when shortly after he may have to recall his prayer, and, as you were saying, demand the opposite of what he at first requested.

SOCRATES: And was not the poet whose words I originally quoted wiser than we are, when he bade us (pray God) to defend us from evil even though we asked for it?

ALCIBIADES: I believe that you are right.

SOCRATES: The Lacedaemonians, too , whether from admiration of the poet or because they have discovered the idea for themselves, are wont to offer the prayer alike in public and private, that the Gods will give unto them the beautiful as well as the good: - no one is likely to hear them make any further petition. And yet up to the present time they have not been less fortunate than other men; or if they have sometimes met with misfortune, the fault has not been due to their prayer. For surely, as I conceive, the Gods have power either to grant our requests, or to send us the contrary of what we ask.

And now I will relate to you a story which I have heard from certain of our elders. It chanced that when the Athenians and Lacedaemonians were at war, our city lost every battle by land and sea and never gained a victory. The Athenians being annoyed and perplexed how to find a remedy for their troubles, decided to send and enquire at the shrine of Ammon. Their envoys were also to ask, 'Why the Gods always granted the victory to the Lacedaemonians?' 'We,' (they were to say,) 'offer them more and finer sacrifices than any other Hellenic state, and adorn their temples with gifts, as nobody else does; moreover, we make the most solemn and costly processions to them every year, and spend more money in their service than all the rest of the Hellenes put together. But the Lacedaemonians take no thought of such matters, and pay so little respect to the Gods that they have a habit of sacrificing blemished animals to them, and in various ways are less zealous than we are, although their wealth is quite equal to ours.' When they had thus spoken, and had made their request to know what remedy they could find against the evils which troubled them, the prophet made no direct answer, - clearly because he was not allowed by the God to do so; - but he summoned them to him and said: 'Thus saith Ammon to the Athenians: "The silent worship of the Lacedaemonians pleaseth me better than all the offerings of the other Hellenes."' Such were the words of the God, and nothing more. He seems to have meant by 'silent worship' the prayer of the Lacedaemonians, which is indeed widely different from the usual requests of the Hellenes. For they either bring to the altar bulls with gilded horns or make offerings to the Gods, and beg at random for what they need, good or bad. When, therefore, the Gods hear them using words of ill omen they reject these costly processions and sacrifices of theirs. And we ought, I think, to be very careful and consider well what we should say and what leave unsaid. Homer, too, will furnish us with similar stories. For he tells us how the Trojans in making their encampment, 'Offered up whole hecatombs to the immortals,' and how the 'sweet savour' was borne 'to the heavens by the winds;

'But the blessed Gods were averse and received it not. For exceedingly did they hate the holy Ilium, Both Priam and the people of the spear-skilled king.'

So that it was in vain for them to sacrifice and offer gifts, seeing that they were hateful to the Gods, who are not, like vile usurers, to be gained over by bribes. And it is foolish for us to boast that we are superior to the Lacedae-monians by reason of our much worship. The idea is inconceivable that the Gods have regard, not to the justice and purity of our souls, but to costly processions and sacrifices, which men may celebrate year after year, although they have committed innumerable crimes against the Gods or against their fellow-men or the state. For the Gods, as Ammon and his prophet declare, are no receivers of gifts, and they scorn such un-worthy service. Wherefore also it would seem that wisdom and justice are especially honoured both by the Gods and by men of sense; and they are the wisest and most just who know how to speak and act towards

Gods and men. But I should like to hear what your opinion is about these matters.

ALCIBIADES: I agree, Socrates, with you and with the God, whom, indeed, it would be unbecoming for me to oppose.

SOCRATES: Do you not remember saying that you were in great perplexity, lest perchance you should ask for evil, supposing that you were asking for good?

ALCIBIADES: I do.

SOCRATES: You see, then, that there is a risk in your approaching the God in prayer, lest haply he should refuse your sacrifice when he hears the blasphemy which you utter, and make you partake of other evils as well. The wisest plan, therefore, seems to me that you should keep silence; for your 'high mindedness' - to use the mildest term which men apply to folly - will most likely prevent you from using the prayer of the Lacedaemonians. You had better wait until we find out how we should behave towards the Gods and towards men.

ALCIBIADES: And how long must I wait, Socrates, and who will be my teacher? I should be very glad to see the man.

SOCRATES: It is he who takes an especial interest in you. But first of all, I think, the darkness must be taken away in which your soul is now enveloped, just as Athene in Homer removes the mist from the eyes of Diomede that

'He may distinguish between God and mortal man.'

Afterwards the means may be given to you whereby you may distinguish between good and evil. At present, I fear, this is beyond your power.

ALCIBIADES: Only let my instructor take away the impediment, whether it pleases him to call it mist or anything else! I care not who he is; but I am resolved to disobey none of his commands, if I am likely to be the better for them.

SOCRATES: And surely he has a wondrous care for you.

ALCIBIADES: It seems to be altogether advisable to put off the sacrifice until he is found.

SOCRATES: You are right: that will be safer than running such a tremendous risk.

ALCIBIADES: But how shall we manage, Socrates? - At any rate I will set this crown of mine upon your head, as you have given me such excellent advice, and to the Gods we will offer crowns and perform the other customary rites when I see that day approaching: nor will it be long hence, if they so will.

SOCRATES: I accept your gift, and shall be ready and willing to receive whatever else you may proffer. Euripides makes Creon say in the play, when he beholds Teiresias with his crown and hears that he has gained it by his skill as the first-fruits of the spoil: -

'An auspicious omen I deem thy victor's wreath: For well thou knowest that wave and storm oppress us.'

And so I count your gift to be a token of good-fortune; for I am in no less stress than Creon, and would fain carry off the victory over your lovers.

APPENDIX I.

It seems impossible to separate by any exact line the genuine writings of Plato from the spurious. The only external evidence to them which is of much value is that of Aristotle; for the Alexandrian catalogues of a century later include manifest forgeries. Even the value of the Aristotelian authority is a good deal impaired by the uncertainty concerning the date and authorship of the writings which are ascribed to him. And several of the citations of Aristotle omit the name of Plato, and some of them omit the name of the dialogue from which they are taken. Prior, however, to the enquiry about the writings of a particular author, general considerations which equally affect all evidence to the genuineness of ancient writings are the following: Shorter works are more likely to have been forged, or to have received an erroneous designation, than longer ones; and some kinds of composition, such as epistles or panegyrical orations, are more liable to suspicion than others; those, again, which have a taste of sophistry in them, or the ring of a later age, or the slighter character of a rhetorical exercise, or in which a motive or some affinity to spurious writings can be detected, or which seem to have originated in a name or statement really occurring in some classical author, are also of doubtful credit; while there is no instance of any ancient writing proved to be a forgery, which combines excellence with length. A really great and original writer would have no object in fathering his works on Plato; and to the forger or imitator, the 'literary hack' of Alexandria and Athens, the Gods did not grant originality or genius. Further, in attempting to balance the evidence for and against a Platonic dialogue, we must not forget that the form of the Platonic writing was common to several of his contemporaries. Aeschines, Euclid, Phaedo, Antisthenes, and in the next generation Aristotle, are all said to have composed dialogues; and mistakes of names are very likely to have occurred. Greek literature in the third century before Christ was almost as voluminous as our own, and without the safeguards of regular publication, or printing, or binding, or even of distinct titles. An unknown writing was naturally attributed to a known writer whose works bore the same character; and the name once appended easily obtained authority. A tendency may also be observed to blend the works and opinions of the master with those of his scholars. To a later Platonist, the difference between Plato and his imitators was not so perceptible as to ourselves. The Memorabilia of Xenophon and the Dialogues of Plato are but a part of a considerable Socratic literature which has passed away. And we must consider how we should regard the question of the genuineness of a particular writing, if this lost literature had been preserved to us.

These considerations lead us to adopt the following criteria of genuineness: (1) That is most certainly Plato's which Aristotle attributes to him by name, which (2) is of considerable length, of (3) great excellence, and also (4) in harmony with the general spirit of the Platonic writings. But the testimony of Aristotle cannot always be distinguished from that of a later age (see above); and has various degrees of importance. Those writings which he cites without mentioning Plato, under their own names, e.g. the Hippias, the Funeral Oration, the Phaedo, etc., have an inferior degree of evidence in their favour. They may have been supposed by him to be the writings of another, although in the case of really great works, e.g. the Phaedo, this is not credible; those again which are quoted but not named, are still more defective in their external credentials. There may be also a possibility that Aristotle was mistaken, or may have confused the master and his scholars in the case of a short writing; but this is inconceivable about a more important work, e.g. the aws, especially when we remember that he was living at Athens, and a frequenter of the groves of the Academy, during the last twenty years of Plato's life. Nor must we forget that in all his numerous citations from the Platonic writings he never attributes any passage found in the extant dialogues to any one but Plato. And lastly, we may remark that one or two great writings, such as the Parmenides and the Politicus, which are wholly devoid of Aristotelian (1) credentials may be fairly attributed to Plato, on the ground of (2) length, (3) excellence, and (4) accordance with the general spirit of his writings. Indeed the greater part of the evidence for the genuineness of ancient Greek authors may be summed up under two heads only: (1) excellence; and (2) uniformity of tradition - a kind of evidence, which though in many cases sufficient, is of inferior value.

Proceeding upon these principles we appear to arrive at the conclusion that nineteen-twentieths of all the writings which have ever been ascribed to Plato, are undoubtedly genuine. There is another portion of them, including the Epistles, the Epinomis, the dialogues rejected by the ancients themselves, namely, the Axiochus, De justo, De virtute, Demodocus, Sisyphus, Eryxias, which on grounds, both of internal and external evidence, we are able with equal certainty to reject. But there still remains a small portion of which we are unable to affirm either that they are genuine or spurious. They may have been written in youth, or possibly like the works of some painters, may be partly or wholly the compositions of pupils; or they may have been the writings of some contemporary transferred by accident to the more celebrated name of Plato, or of some Platonist in the next generation who aspired to imitate his master. Not that on grounds either of language or philosophy we should lightly reject them. Some difference of style, or inferiority of execution, or inconsistency of thought, can hardly be considered decisive of their spurious character. For who always does justice to himself, or who writes with equal care at all times? Certainly not Plato, who exhibits the greatest differences in dramatic power, in the formation of sentences, and in the use of words, if his earlier writings are compared with his later ones, say the Protagoras or Phaedrus with the Laws. Or who can be expected to think in the same manner during a period of authorship extending over above fifty years, in an age of great intellectual activity, as well as of political and literary transition? Certainly not Plato, whose earlier writings are separated from his later ones by as wide an interval of philosophical speculation as that which separates his later writings from Aristotle.

The dialogues which have been translated in the first Appendix, and which appear to have the next claim to genuineness among the Platonic writings, are the Lesser Hippias, the Menexenus or Funeral Oration, the First Alcibiades. Of these, the Lesser Hippias and the Funeral Oration are cited by Aristotle; the first in the Metaphysics, the latter in the Rhetoric. Neither of them are expressly attributed to Plato, but in his citation of both of them he seems to be referring to passages in the extant dialogues. From the mention of 'Hippias' in the singular by Aristotle, we may perhaps infer that he was unacquainted with a second dialogue bearing the same name. Moreover, the mere existence of a Greater and Lesser Hippias, and of a First and Second Alcibiades, does to a certain extent throw a doubt upon both of them. Though a very clever and ingenious work, the Lesser Hippias does not appear to contain anything beyond the power of an imitator, who was also a careful student of the earlier Platonic writings, to invent. The motive or leading thought of the dialogue may be detected in Xen. Mem., and there is no similar instance of a 'motive' which is taken from Xenophon in an undoubted dialogue of Plato. On the other hand, the upholders of the genuineness of the dialogue will find in the Hippias a true Socratic spirit; they will compare the Ion as being akin both in subject and treatment; they will urge the authority of Aristotle; and they will detect in the treatment of the Sophist, in the satirical reasoning upon Homer, in the reductio ad absurdum of the doctrine that vice is ignorance, traces of a Platonic authorship. In reference to the last point we are doubtful, as in some of the other dialogues, whether the author is asserting or overthrowing the paradox of Socrates, or merely following the argument 'whither the wind blows.' That no conclusion is arrived at is also in accordance with the character of the earlier dialogues. The resemblances or imitations of the Gorgias, Protagoras, and Euthydemus, which have been observed in the Hippias, cannot with certainty be adduced on either side of the argument. On the whole, more may be said in favour of the genuineness of the Hippias than against it.

The Menexenus or Funeral Oration is cited by Aristotle, and is interesting as supplying an example of the manner in which the orators praised 'the Athenians among the Athenians,' falsifying persons and dates, and casting a veil over the gloomier events of Athenian history. It exhibits an acquaintance with the funeral oration of Thucydides, and was, perhaps, intended to rival that great work. If genuine, the proper place of the Menexenus would be at the end of the Phaedrus. The satirical opening and the concluding words bear a great resemblance to the earlier dialogues; the oration itself is professedly a mimetic work, like the speeches in the Phaedrus, and cannot therefore be tested by a comparison of the other writings of Plato. The funeral oration of Pericles is expressly mentioned in the Phaedrus, and this may have suggested the subject, in the same manner that the Cleitophon appears to be suggested by the slight mention of Cleitophon and his attachment to Thrasymachus in the Republic; and the Theages by the mention of Theages in the Apology and Republic; or as the Second Alcibiades seems to be founded upon the text of Xenophon, Mem. A similar taste for parody appears not only in the Phaedrus, but in the Protagoras, in the Symposium, and to a certain extent in the Parmenides.

To these two doubtful writings of Plato I have added the First Alcibiades, which, of all the disputed dialogues of Plato, has the greatest merit, and is somewhat longer than any of them, though not verified by the testimony of Aristotle, and in many respects at variance with the Symposium in the description of the relations of Socrates and Alcibiades. Like the Lesser Hippias and the Menexenus, it is to be compared to the earlier writings of Plato. The motive of the piece may, perhaps, be found in that passage of the Symposium in which Alcibiades describes himself as self-convicted by the words of Socrates. For the disparaging manner in which Schleiermacher has spoken of this dialogue there seems to be no sufficient foundation. At the same time, the lesson imparted is simple, and the irony more transparent than in the undoubted dialogues of Plato. We know, too, that Alcibiades was a favourite thesis, and that at least five or six dialogues bearing this name passed current in antiquity, and are attributed to contemporaries of Socrates and Plato. (1) In the entire absence of real external evidence (for the catalogues of the Alexandrian librarians cannot be regarded as trustworthy); and (2) in the absence of the highest marks either of poetical or philosophical excellence; and (3) considering that we have express testimony to the existence of contemporary writings bearing the name of Alcibiades, we are compelled to suspend our judgment on the genuineness of the extant dialogue.

Neither at this point, nor at any other, do we propose to draw an absolute line of demarcation between genuine and spurious writings of Plato. They fade off imperceptibly from one class to another. There may have been degrees of genuineness in the dialogues themselves, as there are certainly degrees of evidence by which they are supported. The traditions of the oral discourses both of Socrates and Plato may have formed the basis of semi-Platonic writings; some of them may be of the same mixed character which is apparent in Aristotle and Hippocrates, although the form of them is different. But the writings of Plato, unlike the writings of Aristotle, seem never to have been confused with the writings of his disciples: this was probably due to their definite form, and to their inimitable excellence. The three dialogues which we have offered in the Appendix to the criticism of the reader may be partly spurious and partly genuine; they may be altogether spurious; - that is an alternative which must be frankly admitted. Nor can we maintain of some other dialogues, such as the Parmenides, and the Sophist, and Politicus, that no considerable objection can be urged against them, though greatly overbalanced by the weight (chiefly) of internal evidence in their favour. Nor, on the other hand, can we exclude a bare possibility that some dialogues which are usually rejected, such as the Greater Hippias and the Cleitophon, may be genuine. The nature and object of these semi-Platonic writings require more careful study and more comparison of them with one another, and with forged writings in general, than they have yet received, before we can finally decide on their character. We do not consider them all as genuine until they can be proved to be spurious, as is often maintained and still more often implied in this and similar discussions; but should say of some of them, that their genuineness is neither proven nor disproven until further evidence about them can be adduced. And we are as confident that the Epistles are spurious, as that the Republic, the Timaeus, and the Laws are genuine.

On the whole, not a twentieth part of the writings which pass under the name of Plato, if we exclude the works rejected by the ancients themselves and two or three other plausible inventions, can be fairly doubted by those who are willing to allow that a considerable change and growth may have taken place in his philosophy (see above). That twentieth debatable portion scarcely in any degree affects our judgment of Plato, either as a thinker or a writer, and though suggesting some interesting questions to the scholar and critic, is of little importance to the general reader.

APPENDIX II.

The two dialogues which are translated in the second appendix are not mentioned by Aristotle, or by any early authority, and have no claim to be ascribed to Plato. They are examples of Platonic dialogues to be assigned probably to the second or third generation after Plato, when his writings were well known at Athens and Alexandria. They exhibit considerable originality, and are remarkable for containing several thoughts of the sort which we suppose to be modern rather than ancient, and which therefore have a peculiar interest for us. The Second Alcibiades shows that the difficulties about prayer which have perplexed Christian theologians were not unknown among the followers of Plato. The Eryxias was doubted by the ancients themselves: yet it may claim the distinction of being, among all Greek or Roman writings, the one which anticipates in the most striking manner the modern science of political economy and gives an abstract form to some of its principal doctrines.

For the translation of these two dialogues I

am indebted to my friend and secretary, Mr. Knight.

That the Dialogue which goes by the name of the Second Alcibiades is a genuine writing of Plato will not be maintained by any modern critic, and was hardly believed by the ancients themselves. The dialectic is poor and weak. There is no power over language, or beauty of style; and there is a certain abruptness and agroikia in the conversation, which is very un-Platonic. The best passage is probably that about the poets:--the remark that the poet, who is of a reserved disposition, is uncommonly difficult to understand, and the ridiculous interpretation of Homer, are entirely in the spirit of Plato (compare Protag; Ion; Apol.). The characters are ill-drawn. Socrates assumes the 'superior person' and preaches too much, while Alcibiades is stupid and heavy-in-hand. There are traces of Stoic influence in the general tone and phraseology of the Dialogue (compare opos melesei tis...kaka: oti pas aphron mainetai): and the writer seems to have been acquainted with the 'Laws' of Plato (compare Laws). An incident from the Symposium is rather clumsily introduced, and two somewhat hackneyed quotations (Symp., Gorg.) recur. The reference to the death of Archelaus as having occurred 'quite lately' is only a fiction, probably suggested by the

Gorgias, where the story of Archelaus is told, and a similar phrase occurs; -ta gar echthes kai proen gegonota tauta, k.t.l. There are several pass- ages which are either corrupt or extremely ill-expressed. But there is a modern interest in the subject of the dialogue; and it is a good example of a short spurious work, which may be attributed to the second or third century before Christ.

Printed in the United States
66643LVS00002B/50

9 781595 404442